MW00810301

6000 DAYS OF US

GOOD DAYS OF US

6000 Days of Us

by
Rosina Rucci

6000 DAYS OF US
by Rosina Rucci

Copyright © 2014 by Rosina Rucci

All Rights Reserved

No part of this publication may be reproduced in any form or by any means, including scanning, photocopying, or otherwise without prior written permission of the copyright holder.

I have tried to recreate events, locales and conversations from my memories of them. My memories may not be accurate, and others may have different recollections of the events and conversations. In some instances, to maintain some individuals' anonymity I have changed the names of individuals and places, and I may have changed some identifying characteristics and details such as physical properties, occupations and places of residence.

ISBN-13: 978-0-9960536-9-3

ISBN-10: 0996053697

~~~~~~

6000 Days of Us may be a quick read, but it's loaded with passion and filled with haunting prose. Rosina Rucci is every woman in love, with details from childhood about her friendship and then romance with Salvatore Testa. After 30 years of silence, Rucci lays bare her soul and tells a gut-wrenching story that both heals and humanizes our aching hearts. This book is proof, once and for all, that love is highly complicated and, when deep and real, survives even death. *6000 Days of Us* will unshackle you.

Cheryl Wills
Author, *Die Free: A Heroic Family Tale*
Broadcast Reporter, NY 1

~~~~~~

6000 Days of Us is the culmination of Rosina Rucci's thirty-year effort to work through the aftermath of her life's greatest love and loss. It is at once entertaining, vivid and ultimately horrifying to realize what these two young people in love lived. A triumphant ending will make your heart soar.

Sara Canuso
President
Women That Influence.

~~~~~~

A deeply sad but ultimately triumphant love story of two young people facing enormous challenges in their lives and love for each other. Rucci writes with bravery and honesty; and the depth of love between her and her beloved is inspiring. This story is proof that true love never dies.

Gina Casella
President,
AT Escapes

This work is dedicated . . .

To Salvatore, my beautiful once and forever Prince, who taught me every single important thing I'd need to know in this life . . .

To Luca, my sweet, beloved child who needed to know what lived in his mother's heart . . .

To Ralph, my brilliant brother so full of heart and goodness, whose undying and unconditional love and support are my breath . . .

In our sleep, pain which cannot forget falls drop by drop upon the heart until, in our own despair, against our will, comes wisdom through the awful grace of God.

~ Aeschylus ~

Not even all the love in the world can change the course of another's destiny.

~ Elsa Morante ~

FOREWORD

I AM NOT A WRITER, nor would I hold myself out to be. I've never written anything but for my own private use. Still and all, I've been writing what follows ahead on these pages for thirty years in my head, retelling myself these stories over and over so as to never forget one single precious detail. I've always thought that it is a story that should be told and that, in its telling, there would be some kind of closure, an ending of the circle, a point at which I could and would arrive where I would realize and begin to really fathom, in the aftermath, what I lived and what I lost. During this process, I did have an epiphany and I did come to understand much more deeply the significance of my love and the many events I lived.

For three decades, I've carried this story inside of me, ambivalent about sharing even a small fraction of it with anyone because I knew this Pandora's box kept buried so deeply in my heart, once opened, would never be closed again. I wished to live with my thoughts and my memories alone because, in truth, I was never alone; in truth, I shared it all with him and only him. But, that all changed when my son was sixteen and I, from one moment to the next, realized that, although he knew what comprised every cell of my being and body, he had no idea what I kept locked up so tightly inside of my heart.

And so here is my story—the story of my deep and never-ending love for a man lost far too soon but whose presence in my soul and whose spiritual essence I carry with me still. Know that this is not a story "based in truth"; rather, it is all true. Every situation described, every conversation, every person actually existed. It is all true.

My story has taught me many things but, above all, I know that a significant, strong love never dies, nor do truly loving relationships end. He is as present as he has ever been; even if I do not see him,

I most certainly do feel him. Also, I wished to honor the man I love who, I believe, died with a dignity that no one knew but me.

I do not wish to judge or blame anyone for any reason. Forgetting is not at all possible and, in most cases, forgiveness isn't even on the table—although I work hard on that, because all of the people who had a part in this story lost far more than can ever be calculated. It was on this level playing field that I have attempted to write each phrase from a place in my heart where there is only love.

Rosina Rucci

ONE

O N MONDAY, OCTOBER 14, 2013, *I hear the clock chime at two in the morning and then a knock on my bedroom wall—three little rapid-fire knocks. I am lying on my right side; the knocks are on the wall behind me. Then I feel a weight on the bed at my back and I feel pressure on the left side of my body, which was facing the ceiling. At first the "hands" are still; then they slowly run up and down the length of my body. I feel him getting settled in right behind me and an energy, both a pressure up against my entire body from my head to my feet and a wild tingling—like an electrical current that covers every inch of me. I don't move a single piece of a single muscle, nor am I afraid.*

Once he stops moving I whisper, "Sal, it's you, I know it's you," and he blows softly into my left ear, "Sssshhhh." I want to turn around but know that if I do, he'll be gone in a second, so I remain perfectly still.

Then he puts his "left arm" over my body and his "hand" right into mine. I take it and wrap my fingers through each of his and squeeze his hand tightly and we stay that way for a few moments, not moving.

He says, "I'm sorry, I'm so sorry.'

I say, "I love you," and he responds: "I love you." I don't hear his words, mind you—he cannot speak. I *feel* his words, if that makes sense.

I look at his hand and it is a full, human hand—all flesh, skin and bones. I even see his fingernails and note that they are a little long. I think, Oh, he must not bite his nails anymore, *and then I close my eyes, continuing to hold his hand and feel the electrical current up and down the back of me. After a few moments I open them again and see that his hand is transparent—just an outline through which I see my night table, but it still holds tightly on to mine.*

'Don't go, don't go," I say, and as he disappears—not suddenly but, rather, as though he were a strip of wax being torn off me—he says, "I'm here; I'm always here," and then he's gone.

TWO

IN THE SUMMER OF 1969, when I was thirteen, I had a terrible crush on my girlfriend Joannie's cousin Michael. He was a shy, serious boy who had a gorgeous, chiseled face, disheveled hair, and a quick smile. I was consumed with thoughts of him. Joannie liked some guy, Salvatore, whom I did not know but knew was friends with Michael. And so it was that we all found ourselves at the Jersey shore, where all of our parents either owned or rented beach houses, with a plan to go and play miniature golf on the boardwalk in Ventnor.

Joannie, Michael, and I went to meet Sal on the boardwalk, not far from where he lived. Even though it was dark I could see that he was good-looking. Michael said, "Rosina, this is Salvie Testa."

All I managed was a perfunctory "hi" and he immediately started to act like a clown, cracking jokes and suggesting we "go to the playground and 'play.'" I thought, *What a conceited jackass*. We went to play miniature golf and the more the evening wore on, the more adorable I thought he was. Actually, I thought he was pretty gorgeous. He seemed quite tall—maybe a head over me. Just a few years later, I would see that he was tall enough for me to slip my shoulder under his arm and have it fit tightly into place. He had light brown hair streaked with some blonde—in those days he surfed quite a lot and was in the sun all the time, at least in summer. Several years later I would love to bury my nose in his soft, silky hair that always smelled like Johnson's Baby Shampoo. His dark brown eyes drooped slightly on the corners toward his temples and were framed by brows that had a natural arch, so he always looked surprised—eventually, looking into his face as much as I did for so many years, I would realize that his eyebrows had the natural shape of a ram's horns. His face was round and full and he had fleshy cheeks which I later would love to chew.

His mouth was small but his lips were thick, soft as cotton balls, and I would eventually love the feel of them on my face, lips, neck, and body. That night in Ventnor, New Jersey, all I knew was that he made fun of every bad shot I made. We laughed constantly through the whole ordeal. We went for ice cream after golf and quieted down a bit and then they walked me home later that night. By the next day, I never again thought of Michael.

I do not remember myself at that point in my life . . . all I can tell you is that laughter was and still is my life-force, the one thing that helped me fight my huge shyness. From the beginning, Sal knocked down that wall—from that very first night in the summer of 1969 on the Ventnor boardwalk.

It wasn't until the following year—April 1970—that my family and I moved into the house three doors down from his in South Philadelphia and I saw him again. Our friendship then had a chance to begin. Over the next five or six years, we became best friends who just happened to be a boy and a girl. We were pretty much inseparable, hanging out with his old neighborhood buddies—guys who worked really hard already at that young age, who came from families of far less means than Sal's.

In the early part of his childhood, Sal lived with his family in what is now known as the Italian Market neighborhood—back then, it was just Ninth Street. The neighborhood's center was and still is a seven-block-long open-air food and dry-goods market. All of the food businesses were owned by Italians, founded by immigrants who settled in that old neighborhood and still going strong three generations later, mostly in the same families. All of the dry-goods businesses were initially owned by Jewish people but over time, they all left, selling their businesses first to Asians who in turn sold to Latinos. Today the neighborhood is considered quite desirable, but way back then, even when Sal was little, it was a tough place to grow up. The parish church there is Saint Paul's; there once was also a parochial school of the same name, which Sal attended as a small boy.

THREE

IN THE OPENING SCENE of the film *West Side Story*, the camera presents a bird's-eye view of Hell's Kitchen. You see all of these buildings coming into focus through the clouds and then the camera gets closer and closer down to the street level and the schoolyard. That's how I picture South Philadelphia in my mind's eye, at least when attempting to explain it to someone. It is a seemingly simple but deceptively complex infrastructure of neighborhoods that are far less dense than Hell's Kitchen. Our streets, where people live in row houses, are far more narrow and we have a bit more green. But the spirit of the place is the same—the intense physical proximity of all different kinds of people from all walks of life. Even now, more than a hundred years after the beginning of the first wave of southern Italian immigrants, the neighborhood holds fast and is strongly Italian.

Everyone knows everyone else here; no one's business is ultimately private or sacred. It's all out there for the world to see and hear and know and sometimes even experience all together. I have always believed that these tight little streets are filled with stories of great drama and heroics and we all know some of them. Some of the best people I have ever known come from these streets—most of them are not very highly educated, but they all hold Ph.D.s in Street Smarts and Wisdom.

In this neighborhood, one of your neighbors might be a postman, another a shopkeeper, another a bricklayer, and another a mob guy. We all know each other. While we may maintain distances, we respect each other and we do not judge. There is a certain—almost always unspoken—understanding among us all that cannot be touched or challenged. While I may get up at four-thirty to get to my construction job and you may get up at eleven to go to your clubhouse and accept guests and visitors asking favors all day, there is no resentment, there is no distaste. We know that people have always done this job and it used to be that occasionally those who did this job contributed greatly to the health of the community at large. It does not really phase those of us outside of that world that we are, at all times, so close to it. It only becomes a big deal the day someone from outside our little universe comes in and attempts to challenge our order. Sometimes the challenge comes from within and then we're thrown into a tailspin and we've no idea what to do or how to react. That is something that creates an enormous disturbance and imbalance in the ecosystem of the neighborhood.

This is what happened in those years—an emotional tailspin that lasted from 1980 until 1988. It resulted from the extraordinary challenges that developed from within our little community—a big storm, one event after another, all of which affected the course of the history of this little neighborhood and of my life. But it would be years—long after the dust had settled and I was able to see more clearly what had happened to all of us—before I would understand what had happened.

My father, Emanuel, whose father had a butcher shop on Twelfth and Daly Streets, used to talk about the old "Moustache Petes," as they were called in the old days—the guys who were part of the "Black Hand" of the neighborhood. My grandfather, walking down the street past what was then their hangout, holding my young father's hand, would say, "Emanuel, always say hello. Always be respectful; don't get too close. Keep your distance, but always treat them with kindness and never talk about them to anyone."

That's what it was in this neighborhood, what it may be even to this day. Is it wrong? Is it unjustifiable? This was how the structure of our neighborhood and our lives were set up. We were taught to believe that we really were all "in this together"—all in the same boat, sturdy and solid or fragile and full of holes as it may have been.

My father, who never said a word of disapproval about my relationship with Salvatore, I know was terrified for me but, at the very same time, he loved Sal and loved his father more than he could ever say. I believe in my heart that if you don't come from this neighborhood, if you didn't have people like them near where you grew up, you cannot possibly understand this concept. Our mothers had a huge friendship, Sal's Mom and mine. My dad saw Sal's dad, whom I called "Mr. T," every Friday night on Ninth Street at the Italian Market when my dad would make his "collections." He had a wholesale meat business in addition to his retail store and provided all of the butcher shops on Ninth Street with their meats. The butchers had all known Mr. T. from childhood because they all grew up together and lived where they worked. And so it went, always, the overlapping of worlds, the complications of life, the nearness of something that so wasn't your family culture but was still a part of who you were on so many levels. These are elements of our South Philadelphia lives that no federal prosecutor or DA or judge or FBI agent has ever understood—the closeness, the friendships, and the genuinely positive spirit that existed between people like Sal and his dad and those slightly different from them.

People like my Sal and his dad looked after people like my dad, who worked like an animal six days a week, thirteen hours a day. They never looked down or disrespected people like my dad because they understood the difficulties and challenges they faced. In this neighborhood, we all understand so much from so young an age that discussion is sometimes completely superfluous. This is why, when the horrors began and the TV cameras and the law started showing up, no one ever said anything negative about people like my Sal or his dad or his Godfather. This was who we—all of the "we"—were and we have always strongly resented having our concepts of community challenged from the outside.

Once the horrors and murders in broad daylight began, everything shifted and became something else. It was in all of that conflict that I found myself filled with fear that, over time, turned to a paralyzing terror. My need to make a break was diametrically opposed to Sal's total inability to do so and therein lay our conflict.

In this neighborhood people are not one-percenters—far, far from it. They are not well connected to anyone but each other, mostly. They tend to be office workers, city employees, policemen, firemen, union guys, shopkeepers and number-writers. Well, we used to have a lot of number-writers—I've no idea what those kinds of guys do now. My dad's little butcher shop—off the corner of Twelfth and Wolf—had its resident number-writer (as all little street-corner shops did), a sweet, soft-spoken guy I loved as a kid. His name was Philip d'Amore (Philip of Love). Sometime in the 1930s he had worked as a driver for an equally as young Angelo Bruno, earning his stripes when he drove a big truck all the way up to the Canadian border to load it up with whiskey and drive it all the way back. Alone. His nickname was actually Rep— and, yes, that is what I called him. Please don't ask me what the connection may have been between the two names, because I've never known. Anyhow, his "job" was to sit in my dad's shop all day and take bets from customers who came in and out, from seven AM until closing. He was a hugely funny and spirited character who wore a straw boating hat that was so old it was all torn apart but scotch-taped together. His wife, Madeline, was a classic beauty, not at all like him; while he was a diamond in the rough, she was a pure, sparkling, and polished stone. She had a regal bearing, a long Roman nose, almond-shaped eyes, high cheekbones, and thick, long, very black hair. She set the standard for my concept of Italian feminine beauty, which pretty much holds fast until today. Once in a while, and ever more often now, you'll find a physician or a lawyer or an educator in the neighborhood, but all in all South Philadelphia is known for the simplicity of its people. These are people who get up every day not for themselves but for their families; sometimes they face enormous daily difficulties, but they still muster the courage to go on and with a great sense of humor and even a certain sense of joy. They tend to be heroic and strong without even realizing it.

I moved away from Philadelphia in 1992, when I wanted to be inconspicuous and anonymous. Rome had always been home for me, so that is where I went. During that time, I learned that it is very true what Maya Angelou once said—"You can't leave home. You take it with you everywhere you go." I did that by taking Sal with me in my heart and speaking to him, reaching for him whenever I needed his support, which in those early days in Rome was quite frequently. I've continued to do that for thirty years. Moving back to the States in 2003—to New York—proved to be a huge challenge for me: The detachment of life, of the people there, the big buildings with everyone in his or her "slot," the lack of real human contact, the difficulty of forming interpersonal relationships, the impossibility of healthy communication, as I define the concept. The unspeakable solitude, the disconnection, the edginess, the attitude. No one looks into anyone's face. From the first day we lived there, August 1, 2003, I knew it would never be my place but I stayed until my son, Luca, finished middle school because I did not wish to uproot him yet again. In June 2011 I returned home to my wonderful old house in South Philadelphia, the exact point where I began a very long and circuitous journey away from myself, my life, my heartaches, and then right back to them all once again. This time, I'm here on my terms—and only on my terms.

FOUR

S AL'S CLOSEST FRIEND FROM his early years and until the day he died was Frank Dickerman. They had each other's backs unconditionally all their lives and knew they could count on each other no matter what. At fourteen, Frank already worked with his dad, Dave, in the food-service business at the no-longer-standing Spectrum sports arena in South Philadelphia. Sal's other best friend, Nicky Grassia, worked on a tugboat in the Delaware River, out there from early in the morning until after dark no matter the weather. These kids were Sal's backbone, his support. Even if he lost them in his later years as his life took him elsewhere, he never lost them in his DNA. The guys were all great, solid, hardworking, principled kids. All of them "pieces of bread," as we say. Frenchy, Poindexter, Dickerman, Nicky Grassia—I'll never forget any of them, although I can no longer remember Poindexter's real name. That was his nickname because he looked just like the nerdy cartoon character with the big round black glasses.

Sometimes we'd go horseback riding down in New Jersey on Saturdays and Sundays all together, down the shore when the sun was up, down to the old Spectrum to see sports events—we were all huge Sixers fans. My favorite nights were when we'd go to see the Muhammad Ali fights on closed-circuit television at the Spectrum. Salvie loved Ali and was the force behind my growing to love him. I came to recognize him as a great American hero and to know everything about his life and his talent for "dancing." Salvie understood what made Ali such a champion. He used to say that one of the reasons Ali was his hero was that he refused to go fight in Vietnam in 1967 and was completely vilified by the American media for that refusal. He used to say. "Imagine the guts that took—he told the government to go fuck itself and wound up in jail because of it all because he said 'Why should I go to Vietnam and shoot at those Vietnamese people? No Vietcong ever called me nigger.'"

⌐ During those years when Sal and I were just best friends, I dated lots of guys and really liked a few of them. A lot of the guys I dated were his friends (none of the above-named, however) and so we would still all be together. Sal, too, had a few girlfriends who, predictably, did not like me too much. He would always tease me about the guys I dated, making fun of how badly they sometimes acted or just calling them "hamburgers" because he thought they had weak characters. I would laugh at what he'd say but still felt badly for those guys because I knew that what he said was, more times than not, true. Still and all—he with his mostly silly girls and me with all my loser guys—we'd hang out and go to the movies or watch TV or play pool until late at night and invariably wind up together—just me and him walking me home. Since we were neighbors, we always went home last and on our own. Each and every time he'd walk me to my door, we would kiss each other on the cheek and say "Good night, love you." It was love. It was a deeply loving friendship that was so natural and easy and fun. We didn't know, I don't think, that it was love—for us, it was just the best friendship ever, and we both loved it.

On Sundays in South Philadelphia, once the warm, sunny weather started, all of us, thousands of teenagers, would go "down the lakes"—a big city park officially called FDR Park—and have picnics, play Frisbee, smoke pot or not, and just all hang out together, driving around the long circular drive, stopping to see friends. After dark set in, some kids remained and, parked in their cars, would do things with each other they couldn't do in their homes. It was a party atmosphere, pretty wonderful and fun.

FIVE

SALVIE REALLY LOVED TO dance but only after he had a few (like three or four) scotches in him. He loved to dance and sing to the song—whatever song it was—at the same time, but what was so funny about him doing so is that he had absolutely no beat or voice. Now, while I have no voice to speak of, I have always been able to keep a beat and have always been a good dancer. But when we would dance together I would lose my beat because of him and we'd step all over each other and make a huge mess out of it and just wind up screaming with laughter on the dance floor. The absolute best was when we tried to do the jitterbug together—he was a disaster—and of course, once up, he never wanted to sit down.

At all the friends' weddings, he and his good friend Virgil did that crazy Tarantella where they squat all the way down, fold their arms, and kick out their legs. Don't even let me tell you how many times he wound up flat on the floor, laughing uncontrollably. We'd all be standing around him laughing just as hard.

Growing up in South Philly, there were few things we looked forward to more than the Mummers' Parade on New Year's Day. Back then, it started on Broad Street down at Marconi Plaza and then went up Broad Street, around City Hall, and east down Market Street toward the Delaware River. Up until about twenty years ago, only men marched. There are three divisions: the Comics, the Fancies, and the String Bands.

Sal and his friends from the old neighborhood—Tenth and Carpenter—marched as clowns, of course. They painted their faces and wore brightly colored, cheap satin clown suits and hats and carried their dancing umbrellas. They did the "Mummers' Strut" all the way up Broad Street. The Irish and Polish guys in the parade, in those days, would continue down Market Street to Second Street and then go south on Second for the "Two Street" part of the parade, which would then last for another two days, but mostly the Italian guys would turn around at City Hall and walk all the way back home down Broad Street. Almost every year I would walk on the sidewalk from South Philly up to City Hall and then we'd walk back down together.

If you are born in South Philadelphia, it could really only be by a huge accident of the universe that you do not know how to do the Mummers' Strut at birth. It's a little bit like the dance the old-time Second Lines do in New Orleans, but we add a few extra elements. I swear to God I don't think I know more than three people who can't do the dance—and Salvie was one of them. It's all about keeping the beat. He just couldn't do it—and he looked so funny trying. He knew everybody laughed at him, but he did it anyway because he loved it. How much I loved that spirit that was all his. He did what he wanted in any circumstance, just because it suited him. It only made him more fun and way more lovable in every way, at least to me.

After January 1, 1980, he never marched on Broad Street again.

SIX

OVER THE COURSE OF a few years I had several "boyfriends" and liked some of them quite a lot. All of them knew about my friendship with Sal; some of them actually even knew him. Some of those boys did not like that I was such close friends with Sal, but dated me nevertheless.

In any case, the truth is this: I never felt as though any of those guys were my friends; I never felt as comfortable and at ease with any of those guys as I did with Sal. I think they more or less liked me, but just wanted to have a nice girlfriend. We were kids, so what could we have really known? A few of them tried to go past just kissing me, but I never felt I could acquiesce to any of them because of that feeling I had about the lack of friendship, which is what I had with Sal. I was just a girl to those guys, but, to him, I was a best friend *and* a girl. Sal paid attention to who I was, listened to everything I had to say, knew my insecurities and discomforts, and always tried to help me knock them all down.

So I would tell him about my "boyfriends" and what they said or didn't say, what they did or didn't do. I told him everything, my deepest thoughts, my worries—everything I had inside my head at any given moment—and he always listened intently, as I did to him. We shared all of our thoughts and things with each other, me more than he. Isn't that just what best friends do? He was always right there. Just right there. And there was never anything I ever felt I couldn't say to him; there was never a sense that I couldn't be exactly who I was in his presence. Although largely unspoken, I knew that whoever I was and whatever I was, it was perfectly fine with him—and that feeling was completely reciprocated.

When I was just about seventeen, I was head over heels about one of Sal's friends and we dated for maybe six months—but then he met another girl, who would eventually become his first wife. We never broke up, really, we just stopped going out together. Several months later, in April of that year—1973—I asked him to my senior prom and he actually turned me down! Naturally, I cried a couple of oceans. Unbeknownst to me, my mother had told Sal's mother about what had happened; I had no intention of telling Sal because I was so thoroughly embarrassed and feeling like a total loser. One night, we were hanging out and he said, "So, you going to your prom?"

"No, probably not."

"What are you, nuts? You have to go to your senior prom, it's the only important one! Why aren't you going?"

"I just don't want to."

"Nooooo, come on, you have to go. I want to go. Can we go—together me and you? Come on, we'll go together and we'll have a great time."

In that moment, I knew he knew. I knew he knew that I'd been turned down and he didn't want to say so and embarrass me. He knew that I was planning on just not going to the prom rather than face another embarrassment. And that's how it came to be that he asked me to my prom as his date. I wore a light pink satin dress and made him wear a pink tuxedo jacket with black pants. Sometime later, he said, "It had to be love, because I let you force me to wear that ugly pink jacket!" Everyone there loved him, especially all the black guys, because he wasn't some tight-ass suburban papa's boy, he was a hip, smart street kid from South Philadelphia who had charm to give away. He was fun and funny and easy and cool. The following year, when he graduated, he asked me to his prom and I went.

After all of those sweet "good-night-I-love-you-kisses" as "best friends," it was after his prom when we first kissed seriously. We slow-danced together. I remember that when he asked me to dance that night, I said, "Really? You want to dance?" and he gave me one of those looks, rolling his eyes up and twisting up his mouth. So we slow-danced and I remember feeling completely comfortable but yet sensing something new, different, about dancing with him like that. Later that night, when he walked me to my front door and he kissed me for real and hugged me hard. I said, "Wait a minute, Sal, what are you doing?"

"You know all those times I said that I loved you when we would kiss goodnight? Well, I really meant it. Come on, RoRo, how long you gonna make a guy wait? I love you. I mean I really love you."

I told him that I had always really loved him too all these years. And so we kissed. This time for real.

Later that same night in June 1974, we drove down to his house at the shore with a couple of other friends. That was the night I slept with him in his little-boy room and we made love for the first time. I remember that I was nervous but only for a quick, passing moment because it was a very sweet, loving, gentle experience. Afterward we lay awake most of the night just looking at each other.

SEVEN

THE FIRST DREAM *I had of Sal was quite soon after he died.*

His sister and I are in the living room of his house here on Porter Street and we watch him teleport in. He appears just as though he's coming through a teleport in the old Star Trek episodes—all pixelated, with electrical charges bouncing off him until suddenly, there he is—the complete, real Sal. He opens his arms toward us. She goes under one arm and I go under the other and he kisses us both on our foreheads and says, "I'll always be with you. Don't worry, I'll always be here."

EIGHT

SALVIE KEPT A HORSE down in Clementon, New Jersey, at a stable called Cabana Downs. She was an Appaloosa named Apache. She was very beautiful but wild and rambunctious—she wouldn't let anyone ride her but him. He would call her name and approach her softly and then caress her face and kiss her and speak softly to her, and with him she was always calm. You could see that she just loved him. He taught me how to ride down there at Cabanas and would always choose an old, slow horse for me so that I'd be safe (well, safer) and he could control the situation better. We'd get out there on Saturdays and Sundays at around six in the morning and then be out on the trail by seven. This was our usual weekend activity when we were sixteen and seventeen.

Just about every weekend, two men who I knew as Sal's dad's friends were always there -- Frank Sindone and Joseph Ciancaglini. In the city they were always dressed sharply, in shiny suits, lace shirts, and dark sunglasses, but down at the ranch they were full-blown cowboys. Sindone was always quite reserved with me, sweet but not at all effusive, but Ciancaglini was a big, warm, smiling bear of a guy who always hugged me hard. He was very genuinely who he appeared to be and I took to him, always hugging him back just as tightly. Sometimes we'd go right into the woods and just ride for hours with Sindone, Ciancaglini, and a few other guys I didn't really know, but mostly we'd go off by ourselves.

We'd be out on the trails for hours and stop and have a bite around late morning, tying the horses to trees. We talked for hours, it now seems, about how cool it would be to live on a ranch and raise horses. Somewhere out west, of course, Wyoming or some other big-sky country. We talked about how great it would be to wear nothing but jeans and cowboy boots all the time and ride every day. Every time we had that conversation over the course of that year or so we added a new, important element to the scenario, such as what other kinds of animals we'd have and if we'd have acres of apple trees and lots of kids and dogs. We were still only best friends at the time, so there was no funny stuff out there in the woods. I don't even ever remember thinking about that stuff in relation to him, but realize now that he probably thought about it a lot. Sometimes we'd close our eyes under a tree and have a nap before getting back on our horses and continuing on or going back to the stables. Then we'd wash the horses down, brush them, and feed them before getting on our way.

We were so dirty and muddy by the end of those days but would still sometimes stop for dinner down in the countryside before making our way back to Philadelphia. Sometimes we'd go and grab a bite with Sindone and Ciancaglini and I would just listen to them all talk and never say a word. Most of the time, quite honestly, I remember feeling as though I didn't understand anything at all that they were talking about. I do remember laughing a lot—they teased each other and him, always joking and in good humor. Before we left the stables he'd always tell the stable hands, "Make sure you don't let anyone mess with Apache. Don't let anyone ride her." He was afraid of what she might do if she didn't want a persistent person mounting her. They'd say, "Oh, don't worry. She's ok."

One day came the news that someone had mounted Apache and brought her out of the stables and she had gone completely crazy wild, bucking and rearing and trying to throw the guy off. In her hysteria she had gravely hurt herself. Unfortunately, they had to "put her down"—they had to shoot her. Sal was just devastated and so angry that she died for nothing. I don't now remember if we ever went back to those stables again, but I believe that we did not. Ironically, some dozen years later, Sal would be found dead, full of blood and tied up like an animal, rolled up in a dirty blanket on the road right outside of Cabana Downs. I doubt that the guys who left him there knew the importance of that place to him in his younger years—they did not know him back then. But I did.

NINE

WAY BACK WHEN WE were seventeen, Sal had a girlfriend. She was very tiny, pretty, and sweet, had big black doe eyes, and was always smiling. She also had a very unnerving, highly shrill voice and the biggest boobs I had ever seen. She was very possessive of Sal. I am certain that she disliked me from the moment we met but realized that since I was the best friend who just happened to be a girl, we were a package deal, him and me together. So she tolerated me. I understood and always went out of my way to make her more comfortable, but there was just no soothing her.

Sometimes Sal's girlfriend would be at his house and I'd be there too and she'd be talking to his mother—super-fast, with that nails-on-a-blackboard voice, and his mother would turn around, roll her eyes at me, and mouth, "I can't take her. Do something!"—and we'd laugh in front of her. Eventually even Sal started to laugh, and that's when he started to tell me that he too couldn't take her any longer.

Even though we were all only seventeen, she and her mother wanted him to buy her a diamond ring—they were pressuring him to get engaged to her. At seventeen! His mother said, "Sal, you're too young. Don't even think about that or I'll kill you." He was desperate to break it off but he really didn't know what to do. He started to use me as an excuse to avoid taking her out. If she said "Let's go to the movies on Friday night," he would say, "Oh, I can't —I've got something to do with Rosina." Finally he told her that he and I were now going out together and so she and he had reached the end of their road. He only confessed this to me later, after I ran into her on Passyunk Avenue and she exploded at me.

Years later, he used the exact same strategy to alienate the young lady he'd become engaged to—pulling me into the story. I knew exactly what he was doing the second time and was infuriated. He just did not have the stomach for these kinds of confrontations. Sometimes I think he's lucky he died so young, because that is the one reason I have been able to forgive him for everything. And I do mean everything—well, that and the fact that I loved him as much as I did. He never, by the way, *ever* said "I'm sorry" for anything. Never, ever, ever. Except at the end.

TEN

*I*T IS *FEBRUARY* 5, 1997, *and I am in Ospedale Fatebenefratelli in Rome awaiting the birth of my son, Luca. Sal has been dead for thirteen years.*

After a long day of attempts to induce labor with no response from my body, my doctor says he has detected fetal distress and must perform a Cesarean to deliver my child. I am frightened and start to cry. Thankfully, no fewer than a dozen of my friends are there with me and so I also feel comforted.

As I am walking from my labor room into the operating room, I start praying: "Sal, please come now, please stay with me. Please be here with me and let me know you're here now. I am really scared and I need you now." I don't normally speak to God, who I think has enough to worry about, nor do I regularly whisper to any saints. I speak to what I know and what I love and so I speak to Sal in these situations. Always.

Several moments later, I am on the table in the OR and they're prepping me. I am in and out of consciousness but more awake than not. I close my eyes and there he is, his face right over mine.

"I would never let anything happen to you. Don't worry. Don't worry about anything. I'm right here. You think I wouldn't be here? He's going to be fine too."

I melt into the experience—I open my eyes and am as present as I can be, even speaking to the people working on me, and then Luca arrives. Years later, my spiritual advisor will describe the entire scene of Luca's birth in that operating room in Rome to me and say that Sal hovered above and behind my head the entire time.

ELEVEN

I saw Sal's closest friend the other day on the street in South Philadelphia. After more than twenty-five years in prison, he is now free once again.

He was Sal's best friend in that world and I loved him, too. He was (and probably still is) so smart and so sharp and so full of potential and dynamism. In another universe, a guy like him could have gone on and conquered the known world. But, having grown up in South Philadelphia, born into that world, he really had no choice.

About two weeks after Salvie died, I was out to dinner with a few very close friends. After dinner we stopped at the bar to have a nightcap. Suddenly the door opened and in he walked with a few guys. I looked up at him and my stomach just fell to the floor. I watched him zero in on me and walk directly up to me. Without saying a word, he just enveloped me in his arms and held me tightly for I don't even know how long and buried his face in my neck. He didn't speak. When he let go of me, we stood there face to face, silent for a moment. I said, "How are you?"

He shrugged his shoulders, held the palms of his hands up toward the ceiling, and, raising his eyebrows, said, "I'm still here."

I couldn't muster a response. I just froze.

Shortly after that sighting, I had a dream that I was a passenger in a car that he was driving. I knew it was him but his face was obscured by a thick nylon stocking. At first I felt perfectly comfortable sitting next to him and then I said, "Okay, please just tell me how you did it. Please tell me that Salvie didn't know what hit him."

He very calmly, slowly and succinctly began to tell me the story and the deeper he got into the explanation, the more hysterical I became. I forced myself awake before arriving at the end of the story. I had this dream many, many times over the course of many months and actually had to seek the help of a hypnotist to stop its recurrence. It was only almost thirty years later, when I read George Anastasia's book *Blood and Honor*, that I learned that every single detail described to me in the dream actually happened in the back of that little candy store in South Philadelphia where Sal was killed.

In my dream, he always tried to reassure me that Salvie died instantaneously, but I've always believed that he had a flash of awareness before actually dying and that thought caused me great anguish for many years.

TWELVE

S AL HAD A LITTLE motorboat he kept in a slip on the bay in Ventnor, New Jersey. In the summertime, we were always on it. He loved to speed, which made me throw up every time—and Sal would throw up watching me throw up. One time, a friend of his—I think it was Anthony Ferrante, on whom I had an enormous crush—pulled up next to us in this big, macho boat and he and all of his buddies started in: "Yo, Sal, how'd you get that motor on that bathtub you're driving?"

Sal got all kinds of embarrassed and insulted. He was not at all happy that I was laughing, but if you knew him—really, really well—you just couldn't help teasing him, because you knew that no one loved a good laugh, even at his own expense, more than he did.

Back at the dock, as we were hosing down the boat, Sal said, "I gotta get a better boat." Long story short, he did. When the day came for him to take possession, his plan was to drive right to the shore and put it in the water. All he kept talking about was that the new boat had a bathroom—"How cool is that?"

When we got to the boatyard, somewhere on the Black Horse Pike in New Jersey, there it was. It was a light copper color, beautiful, and way bigger than the last one. He said, "We'll do some great skiing on the back of this boat—it's really powerful." He was like a little kid on Christmas morning as the boatyard guy pointed out every special feature.

Finally Sal asked, "And the bathroom—where is it?" We were in the sleeping cabin underneath the deck. The man lifted one of the pillows that comprised the sofa and bed and said, "Here it is." We looked down into the hole—and there was a bucket! The look on Sal's face was beyond priceless. He went white and his chin dropped.

"This is a bathroom?"

"Clearly not," the man replied, "but when you're out on the ocean, if someone needs to go . . . Just empty it out once you get back to the dock."

Sal looked at me and said, "We'll always be the only two people who know that that's there."

All the way to the shore, he just kept saying, "Now remember, nobody else will ever know about that bucket" over and over—and the more he talked about it, the more I laughed.

He named that pretty boat "Alfie" after his mother. We passed a million hours on it and sometimes, laughing like the crazy person he occasionally was, Sal would intentionally drive the boat up onto a sandbar so that we'd be stranded until the tide came in. We passed the time making love down below until the water got higher, and then we'd make our way home.

THIRTEEN

E LOVED TO GO to concerts, too. We saw tons of great performers over the years—Diana Ross, Cher, Sinatra, of course—all fabulous. Our favorite concert ever, though, was Tony Bennett and Lena Horne together at the Academy of Music in Philadelphia. We loved them so much that we followed them to Carnegie Hall in New York to see them a second time. They were both, at the time, coming down from years of hardship over great personal loss and addiction battles, so their support and love for one another as good friends only lent themselves beautifully to their performances.

Over the course of quite a few years between the mid-seventies and early eighties, we saw Frank Sinatra about five times at the old Latin Casino in Cherry Hill, New Jersey, and at Resorts Hotel and Casino in Atlantic City. The first time we saw him in concert, Sal took both his mom and me and I can still remember how excited she and I were. When we got there, there were crazy crowds of people, all clamoring to get into the doors and we were just part of the crush. Sal left us there, in the crowd for a bit, and squished his way into the doors and ahead of everyone and was gone for a few minutes, returning and saying that there was no way we'd wait in that crowd. Moments later, someone came running out to us and waving his hand for us to enter and he began calling "Doctor Testa, Doctor Testa and party, please step right this way," and that's how we got pulled in front of everyone in the crush. The maître'd led us all the way up to the front—the tables radiated out from the stage—but every table in front was already completely full. Next thing we knew, as we were standing there feeling a bit embarrassed, a man carrying a table and three men carrying chairs whisked their way down an aisle and set us up in seconds right in the middle of the aisle. Our embarrassment ended moments later, once the lights went down. Many years later, I saw Scorcese's *Goodfellas* and got very emotional during a scene that played out exactly like this one—when Henry Hill and all his buddies and their girlfriends went to the Copacabana to see Jerry Vale. The truth of that film hit me very, very close to my heart and was—and still is—very difficult for me to watch.

We saw Frank Sinatra about five times in New Jersey. Once we sat in the first two seats (across from each other) at one of the front tables, so I got to rest my elbows on the stage. We were so close to Sinatra that I had to hold my head all the way back in order to see him; at the end of the concert, he greeted a few of us there up in front at the stage. He kissed my cheek and I lost my breath. Naturally, Salvie got a little jealous because that's the way he was.

Another time, we saw Diana Ross at the Latin Casino and again sat at one of the front tables. We adored her—she was amazing and gorgeous that evening and when she came down onto the floor with her microphone, singing "Reach Out and Touch Somebody's Hand," she went to Sal but he waved her away, embarrassed. I, on the other hand, jumped up and immediately started singing, nose to nose with her, and holding her mike with my hand as well. He just looked at me as if to say, "You just had to do it, didn't you?" And of course I did.

FOURTEEN

Y PEOPLE COME FROM Calabria, the toe of the boot, on my mom's side and Abruzzo on my dad's. They are light-years different in culture and character.

The Calabresi take offense at everything, take everything personally, and are somewhat quick to violence; the Abruzzesi are mountain people, sturdy and strong. They live very close to nature and to the land, in the mountains and near the sea, and they take nothing personally. They are almost always peaceful and tranquil and they usually live lives of quiet dignity. The Calabresi and the Abruzzesi couldn't be farther apart in terms of collective character traits.

And then there are the Sicilians. Truly a breed apart.

Three of Sal's grandparents were born in Sicily and no matter how long they lived here before they died, they were all very deeply tied to their homeland. There is no place on earth more beautiful than Sicily or, possibly, quite as fascinating. The Sicilians don't consider themselves Italian—they are Sicilian first and forever. They have an island mentality—they're surrounded by water and they know it and act it. Everything and everyone they don't know is suspect; nothing from the outside is to be trusted; everything and everyone from the outside is to be dealt with very carefully and from a safe distance until that trust is earned. Their loyalty to each other is never to be questioned. Their willingness to look out for one another and "be there" for one another is undisputed; to be accepted into their highly select group, you have to prove that you deserve the honor.

This is a place where the Saracens, the Greeks, the Arabs, the Germans, the Nordics all arrived, some conquering and remaining—everyone came here and believed that they had found Paradise. Truly, they had. One invading force after another helped to create this collective mentality among the indigenous people, who had to protect themselves and their loved ones from these onslaughts over the course of millennia. Some of the strongest and most courageous ones left, crossing the ocean and finding themselves on the streets of the cities of America with the same mentality, the same historical DNA, and the same need to be as they had always been.

Sicilians are also very morose; they are weighed down by their own history, by all the death and destruction and mourning. They're people who move through life with the sense of a heavy dark cloud in their souls. The great journalist Giuseppe Fava once said, *Essere Siciliano significa che hai una lotta eterna fra l'infelicita, la paura e la speranza* ("To be Sicilian means that you fight endlessly with unhappiness, fear and hope").

This was not who Salvatore was at his core but it was who he would eventually become as he transformed and moved deeper and deeper into the dark world of his life. Sal, like his father and grandfather before him, was very old-world. You never, ever turn your back on your family, on your friends. You must stand up and defend them no matter what is before you. You must never cross the line and go against your people. Not ever. No matter what the consequences. He took it all in. And he believed in it. As did his dad. Sadly, not many of their colleagues subscribed to the same lofty principles.

Allow me to digress a moment regarding "loyalty." Sal's dad went to the same barber all his life. The man had a little shop in the old neighborhood. Even after he got older and was declared legally blind, Mr. T continued to go to him and would make Sal go as well. We laughed about that—even Mr. T laughed about it—but he said, "What can I do? I have to keep going until he closes his shop."

Way back in the early part of the twentieth century, we—Southern Italians—short, dark, and swarthy as most of us were, were not at all welcome into this very white world stolen from the Native tribes. We were looked upon with great suspicion and disdain by those outside of our little enclaves. It was up to us to provide a societal structure for ourselves, and that's how this thing of ours took root and grew. My grandfather, who was from a seacoast village in Calabria, worked the coal mines in western Pennsylvania as a young immigrant. He and his fellow Calabresi would leave the mines in the evening and look for a place to have dinner—and everywhere they went there were signs in the windows of the little local diners that said: NO DOGS OR ITALIANS. When this is your reality, when you know you have no one to turn to, when you realize there is no state to back you up, you simply create your own. The police and local authorities wanted nothing to do with us, nor did we want anything to do with them, because we knew they couldn't be trusted. Average people had no alternative but to take care of their own issues and problems in their small, insular world. They did what they had to do. When the government does not exist, when it has no presence, when it provides no recourse for those in need, bad people—people with far less than noble intentions—flourish.

Sicily is also a very patriarchal society—the men rule in absolute and the rules and regulations are endless. In the old days, men commanded and the women were not much more than chattel. I do not know if Sal's grandfather subscribed to this way of thought. I cannot say if he loved his wife, but I believed he did. Sal's grandmother was an exquisitely beautiful little woman with a strong jaw and high, sculpted cheekbones. She wore her thin hair in an aristocratic bun on the crown of her head. She worked right next to her husband, Salvatore, in their poultry store on Ninth and Christian Streets, in the heart of Philadelphia's Italian Market. She had eight children with him, and a day after each birth, she was back on her feet in the poultry store by her husband's side, helping him run their business.

She was tired. I always saw her as very tired. I do not recall that she was a particularly joyful person, even though she always smiled, but I do think she realized how devoted her children and grandchildren were to her. Sal and I would often go and visit her and his three extremely colorful, fun, and loving aunts. We both loved that house of endless activity and (in those days) joy and laughter and a constantly full kitchen table. Grandmom Testa was as tiny as a sparrow and to meet her eye to eye and hold and kiss her, Sal would get down on his knees before her. They were always very loving and tender with each other.

She always knew who he was, even once her dementia set in. She would take him to the side, she no taller than the level of his waist in her little black dress, and, with her finger pointed up at him, would whisper that his grandfather was still alive and that she was angry at him. "Your grandfather left me with all these kids," she'd say. "He left me and went back to Sicily and took up with another woman and now has another family. And me? What can I do with all these kids and no money? You're my grandson, you have to help me." She'd stare off into space and he would get so upset and insist to her that none of that was true—that Grandpop had passed away and that the kids were all grown and that she didn't have to worry about anything.

"Stop fighting her, Sal," I would say to him. "This is what's real for her. Just give her what you've got in your pockets and stop trying to convince her what is real. Just do it, Sal, and quit fighting her. She's already buried two of her children and her husband. If this is what she has to tell herself to get through a day, let her do it. Just give her what she's asking for." Eventually, he calmed down about her deteriorating condition and even joked about it, saying, 'My grandmother's got the best racket going downtown."

Sal's grandmom had followed all the rules and regulations to the letter and I believe, for the most part, so had her daughters, at least while their father was alive. So had Sal's mother, Alfia. And then there was me. Since I was in first grade, all I have ever done is break most every single rule presented to me. I really don't do well with rules and regulations. I've always made my own rules in every situation I've ever been in, as best I can, but Sal couldn't have lived that way. In order for him to live the life he was moving toward well and harmoniously, he needed for me to follow the patriarchal order of things and defer to him and to his dad, to become the beloved but lesser-than in the household. That's what I would have had to do in order to make for a happy home. As much as I loved him, as much as I loved his dad, as much as I wished I could attempt to make up for the eventual loss of his mother (which never would have been possible), those rules were something I knew I could never follow. He knew it, too, but in our early years, that wasn't a conflict for us at all. The conflict came later, with the massive changes that occurred in Sal's life as he moved toward his destiny.

FIFTEEN

*S*ATURDAY, APRIL *13, 2013 I awaken to the feeling of a strong electrical current hovering over the top of my body, from my neck to my feet—an indescribably powerful tingling. We are making love—passionately and with exuberance and as I reach climax I say, "It's you, it's you, I know it's you." As I speak those words, I awaken immediately and as soon as I do, he's gone.*

A few moments earlier, I dream that I am outside, hosing down my dusty sidewalk and I look up and see an old, bent man walking toward me. As he gets closer, he transforms—he slowly stands taller, more erect, his hair gets fuller and darker, and suddenly he is smiling at me. He comes to me and takes me into his arms and hugs me tightly and kisses me. I feel happy and say, "Oh, you're so happy to see me. Do you still love me?" He looks at me and, squeezing my two cheeks in his hands, says, "Look how connected we are. Don't you know how connected we are? Don't you know? I'm always here and I'll never leave you." And then we are in bed.

SIXTEEN

S AL TAUGHT ME HOW to drive a manual-shift car—I learned on his old pumpkin-colored Corvette, which his dad bought him when he turned seventeen. The day it arrived, a few of his dad's friend drove up in it and started beeping the horn. Sal and his dad came out of the house and suddenly there was a party in the street. We were all laughing and having a great time over his reaction—he was hugging and kissing all of those guys—and then, of course, he and I got in and off we went, all around South Philadelphia.

He wanted to teach me how to drive it, so we would go down near the old Food Center, where the streets were wide, when it was almost totally deserted. Of course, until I got the feel of a clutch, I almost crashed into trucks and cyclone fences a thousand times. One time he set up cardboard boxes in the middle of the street and told me to snake through them. Once he was out of the car, I did the snake thing, not stalling once—and then took off and left him there. When I came back for him after maybe ten minutes, he was mad, but he was laughing. I cannot recall one single time in all of our years when he ever got really mad at me.

The Corvette met with an untimely death one summer, at four-thirty in the morning in Atlantic City. He only had it for about two or three years. Anyway, we had been out at the clubs that Saturday night, dancing and drinking in rounds with various groups of friends; about four AM, we got into the car to drive to Sal's house at the shore in Ventnor to sleep.

Now, Pacific Avenue is the last street before the boardwalk and the beach. At each intersection there is a mound of asphalt, on top of which is a culvert. At that hour the red lights were just blinking, suggesting that maybe you'd like to slow down, but naturally Sal was flying.

I yelled at him, "Sal, you will get us both killed if you don't slow down! Don't you see those mounds on every corner?"

No sooner had I said it than we hit a really big one head-on and the car flew straight up into the air, right off the ground. It felt like a carnival ride for a few seconds until it suddenly slammed down onto the ground and came to a full stop with a crash. He looked at me and said, "Oh, Christ, I think the bottom of the car just fell out." I didn't even understand what that meant until he tried and tried and tried to restart the car but all it did was choke. We started to laugh and laugh and we did not stop, not even when he got behind the car to push it and I steered it into the parking lot of some cheap motel on the side of the street. All the while he kept repeating, "Here's where my father kills me. My father's going to kill me for this. I'm going to die for this." The more he talked, the more I laughed and the more I laughed, the more he laughed, all the while repeating, "This really isn't funny."

We wound up leaving the car there (I never did see it again and I don't think he did, either) and walked home three miles down the boardwalk, laughing all the way, carrying my heels—stopping every so often to sit on a bench and to watch how beautifully the sky's colors were transforming with the onset of dawn.

SEVENTEEN

ONE NIGHT, MAYBE A year or two after Sal's death, I am in my apartment on Tenth Street in the old Italian Market. I have a cat, a gorgeous Persian named Tito who is as big as a Buick. She is huge and gorgeous and I love her.

I have just gotten into my bed, to the right of which is the outside wall of the house. Right by the footboard of the bed is the window, which looks out onto the backyard. I hear Tito crunching her kibbles and lapping up some water before coming to bed. All of a sudden, she comes flying across the bedroom—from the door, she leaps onto my bed and bounces right back up and lands on the windowsill. She turns around and faces the door, all rigid and wide-eyed. Just as I think "What the hell happened to Tito?" I hear not feet, but the sound of a hand slapping my linoleum kitchen floor five times. I freeze.

Mind you, I am on my right side with my back to the bedroom door, and I am frozen with fear. I hear footsteps moving across the kitchen floor and then across the living-room carpet. Tito is as frozen as I am, stiff, rigid as a stone.

I feel a weight on the bed at my back and then two hands slide my comforter under me, very slowly, and put it in place. I am so frightened that I say, "Oh, please, Sal, I'm way too scared. I can't handle this, please don't do this." In that very same split second his presence is gone. Then and only then does Tito's body relax; she jumps onto the bed and falls asleep.

This isn't a dream, mind you, because I am completely and totally wide awake.

EIGHTEEN

WHEN SAL'S DAD CAME up through the ranks of his organization, it was under the reign of a man named Angelo Bruno. Mr. Bruno was called the "Gentle Don" because Philadelphia did not have the violence and distress and strife of other cities. The business appeared to be based primarily on gambling, in all of its forms: numbers, loan sharking, card games, sports betting, and so on. The billion-dollar world of drugs was not yet present, nor would the Don wish to have anything to do with it later. There was more than enough for everybody to live on and to share.

Sal loved the old-world mentality of his father and Godfather. He believed in that life and its standards. Later, like a soldier, he was thrust into a whirlwind of circumstances beyond his control; the old standards were disintegrating and a new type of individual was emerging in that world. This was a struggle for Sal; in his humanity and youth, he found himself trying to straddle these two worlds, with one foot in each. A perfect balance would prove impossible to achieve in the long term.

I often think about why Mr. Bruno is still the stuff of myth in Philadelphia. I knew him and his wife, whom Sal called 'Aunt Sue'. She was a petite woman, fair-skinned and blonde, who had an enormous spirit and was very gregarious. The first time I met her, at Sal's house, she was wearing light-pink suede high-heels and the most beautiful gold charm bracelet I'd ever seen. I remember trying hard not to stare at her feet and wrist, but I was very intrigued. Those shoes and that bracelet, to me, spoke of her uniqueness. These two people were, individually and together, highly cultured, beautiful, brilliant, very dynamic and charismatic people. They were avid readers, went to the theater, had friends across the globe, loved the opera, summered in

Sicily—their world was open and their lives were widely and deeply lived, or so it seemed to me from the outside. Mr. B was nothing if not "old world," and Sal's father followed in his footsteps and raised Sal accordingly. Drugs were poison to be avoided. Period. Sal never got high in his whole life. He never smoked a joint or took a pill. Never. Once I saw him try to smoke a cigarette: after two puffs, he choked for ten minutes.

Once Mr. B was gone, greed and the lust for power set in and everything changed. The younger ones coming up held fast to none of the ancient traditions, the history. Their greed was already part of their DNA. Did Sal also have that? I do not believe he did. Sure, he wanted to make money and have all the trappings, but he did not wish to live his life in a flashy, ostentatious way. He was very conscious of the "codes of behavior" imposed on him and his life by the older men and he followed them, respected them, and was embarrassed by certain of his contemporaries who did not. In this midst of all this disturbance to the sociological order of things, I believed that as long as his father was alive they could have maintained a bit of control, but once Mr. T was gone, that was also the beginning of the end for Sal as well—at least, for me. After his father's death Sal said to me, "I didn't just lose my father, Rosina—my whole world has been destroyed." He thoroughly understood the ramifications of that loss in the exact moment it occurred, even if its magnitude had yet to unfold itself fully.

Mr. Scarfo, who took over later, didn't have "men" around him. He surrounded himself with kids—kids off the street, who, more likely than not, out of great fear did anything he wanted them to do. These young guys weren't raised by older men who followed the code; they had no sense of history, they had no concept of any traditions or the old standard of honor and respect, only a dog-eat-dog mentality that eventually shoved them all up against a wall. Most of all, I think, they had fear.

I ask myself now if I saw a ruthlessness in Sal then. I eventually did, as I watched him slowly transform over the course of those many years, and this was the fundamental reason I too transformed and began slowly to distance myself from him. I loved him, deeply and always, and wanted to remain with him forever—but once I began to feel fear, I was never again able to shake it or rationalize it or pretend that it wasn't there. It had too strong a grip on my heart. It became its own entity as it grew inside me.

Had he gotten out when I was imploring him to, he might have been able to change the course of his destiny. But getting out was never an option for him, and, truth be told, he didn't want to get out because he loved that life because, quite honestly, there is so much to it that is irresistible for a man.

Years later, after he had come full circle in his transformation, after all of the horror and loss, he said to me, "I apologize for everything. I should have listened to you because all of these years you were right. You were right about everything and everyone." As he spoke, that last night we were together before he died, I looked into his eyes and I saw the depth of his sincerity, sorrow and regret.

NINETEEN

E WENT SKIING ONCE, when we were maybe seventeen or eighteen. We drove up to Jack Frost Mountain in the Poconos in the Corvette with a ton of other kids one Saturday or Sunday morning, leaving way before daybreak. Of course, we didn't have waterproof clothes—who in South Philly in those days had waterproof clothes? We were in jeans and leather and cowboy boots, like always. We got on the lift and started going up the mountain and Sal looked at me and said, "What the fuck did we do this for? Can you believe that we got up at four AM, drove two hours in the dark to get here, paid all that money to put on all this equipment, and now we have to go down this fucking mountain and put our lives in danger?" We laughed so hard our gondola shook. Near the end of the ride, I fell off and my skis stuck straight up into the snow. Sal couldn't pull me out and we were screaming laughing, everyone around us no doubt thinking, *Look at those South Philly hoodlums making fools of themselves!*

Finally he pulled me free and we slid to the top of the mountain and looked down.

"We gotta go down this thing on these skis we don't know how to use?"

I said, "Just remember to move them from side to side and if you start going straight, make yourself fall down."

We literally fell down the entire mountain, screaming with laughter the whole way. I may have even peed in my pants—since I was already soaked with snow, it wouldn't have made a difference. I remember losing him on my way down.

Once I reached the bottom, I took off my skis, marched into the clubhouse, got a hot chocolate, and positioned myself in front of the big glass window to watch for him. After only a few minutes, I saw him flying straight down at about 75 miles an hour. *Uh oh, here's where he dies*, I thought—and then he skied *off* the snow and into a pile of rocks. He looked just like the Road Runner in a Wile E. Coyote cartoon, crashing right into the rocks with his face on the side and his arms and legs flailed.

I ran out of the clubhouse to go and see if he was okay. He was bruised and banged up, but as soon as he saw me we started laughing uncontrollably.

"Come on, let's go the fuck home," he said, and we laughed the whole way back to Philly.

TWENTY

HERE'S AN OLD ITALIAN card game called *ziganette*. I'm sure that's not the right word in Italian—this is surely an Italian-American word.

Anyway, the game, which is actually the Sicilian version of poker, was one of the biggest rackets in Philadelphia way back in the mid- to late seventies, before all the horror started. The games were run by a man named Frank "Chickie" Narducci.

I loved Mr. Narducci, as I always called him. Pretty much everyone loved him. Sal and his son Frank were very close friends, and I was quite close with Frank's girlfriend, Sandy. Chickie was a barrel-chested guy with slightly bent ears, a bald head, and a purely handsome face cracked in half, always, by the biggest smile I had ever seen. He was full of warmth, welcome, and generosity. His wife Adeline was the female version of him—very tall and statuesque, not a conventional beauty. Her quick smile, warmth, and openness made her seem quite beautiful to me. Whenever Salvie said "Come on, you wanna go to Frankie's house?" I couldn't wait to put on some lipstick and jump into the car.

Every Christmas Eve they had an open house and people filed in all night long, starting at about six PM and finishing well into the early hours of Christmas morning. She did most of the cooking down in her basement kitchen in Packer Park—you entered by the driveway door. The basement was like a big, open loft space and the food was endless. There were always tons of people and music and joy. Christmas Eve was a party, not a solemn, holy celebration. It was a yet another opportunity to invite a billion people into their home to partake of their food, generosity, and sense of *gioia della vita* and enjoy themselves fully and totally. Naturally, at midnight, Chickie would enter dressed as Santa Claus with a stuffed sack full of presents.

Back to Chickie's ziganette games—the action all happened in a little old converted garage in South Philadelphia somewhere around Seventh and Wharton—who remembers now? I remember walking into a dark doorway—no signage, no light, no nothing—saying, "Sal, where the hell are you taking me?"

"Don't worry. It's Chickie's place. You'll see. Just hold my hand."

The lights inside were dim but after a few moments your eyes got used to it. The space was "no frills"—bare walls, fluorescent lights, cement floors—but the food table was lavish and full of trays of sausage and peppers, roast beef, roast pork, meatballs, broccoli rabe, baked ziti, garlic bread, and salad. There was a cash bar and sweet tables and everybody was playing ziganette at long folding tables—judges, big-name lawyers, politicians, fancy-pants Main Line bankers, WASP-y white-bread types. They all loved our way down here in South Philadelphia and just wanted to be a part of it all. And so they were.

The action was nonstop and the noise and din were sometimes unbearable, with all the people shouting and screaming and piped-in music in the background. As we walked from table to table Salvie would say to me, "Don't move a muscle on your face, don't look at anybody's cards and make an expression, because you should never let anyone know what you're thinking. You might see somebody lay down five or ten thousand dollars on one card—don't ever show you care. Don't flinch." Not so easy for me, that, but I did it. He knew almost everyone in the place and I just loved meeting all of these people from all walks of life. Salvie played a bit and I just watched but I was happy to be there the two or three times I went with him. The atmosphere was very nightclubby—lots of music, Sinatra, the classics, and the people were all very spirited and jovial and totally in the moment.

In the middle of it all, on top of a huge ladder maybe twelve feet high, Chickie watched over all the activity. In those days there was no closed-circuit surveillance—at least not in a garage in South

Philadelphia. Then, invariably, after hours of the guys handing him plates of food and drinks up there on that ladder, he'd get blasted and come down and sing. All the action would stop and the whole crowd would just silently and happily indulge him. It was pretty magical. The first time I went, Chickie sang "Pennies from Heaven" and every time he sang the title, all the people in the crowd threw their coins on him.

Every time it rains, it rains pennies from heaven (cue sound: tons of pennies hitting concrete floor)

Don't you know each cloud contains pennies from heaven (cue sound again)

You'll find your fortunes falling all over the town

Just be sure that your umbrella is upside down (and he'd open an umbrella.)

And despite the fact that he couldn't sing worth a damn, the crowd would go bananas, absolutely insane, roaring their cheers and applause.

All of this in South Philadelphia, the richest little neighborhood in the world.

TWENTY-ONE

VERY EARLY ON, MAYBE when we were about twenty-one or twenty-two, I knew Sal was running around on me and we were starting to fight. He was getting more and more cocky. Money, cars, no hours to be home, so beautiful, charming, and fun—to say that girls threw themselves at him would be a grossly understated truth. I was the "official" girlfriend—the one who went out on Saturday nights, the one who had dinner with the family on Sundays, the one who knew, intimately, the grandparents and aunts and uncles and cousins—but suddenly there were lots of others, and it wore me down. I fought with him, my mother fought with him, his mother fought with him—but now I see that it was really all part of the package that life was presenting to him and that he was willingly accepting. It was all very hard for me and the hurt, eventually, ran very deep.

I threw him out of my house a thousand times, cursing at him and throwing things at his back. He never responded. He never got upset. He would just disappear for a couple of days and then come back. He always came back—"RoRo, please. Please. You're the only one." And I melted again and again, time after time, year after year. Sometimes, now, I get really mad at that girl who allowed herself to be subjected to so much, but I would not have been me had I responded in any other way. I knew that I had his heart. I really knew.

We would go out with more or less the same group of guys and their girlfriends. New Year's Eves, dinners at The Saloon in South Philly (still one of the best restaurants *ever*), concerts, shows. The girlfriends were all absolutely fantastic—some of them, even now, are still friends. We had some wonderful and memorable evenings together, and, one by one, each of those couples eventually married.

Meanwhile, I kept thinking that if I could just hang in, eventually he'd grow up and tire of the scene and the swagger and the James Bond existence and begin to calm down. But, as I said, the truth was that Sal loved that life. He thrived on it. He knew he had the world in his pocket because no one looked like him, no one had his charisma, no one attracted people—men and women—the way he did. It really was an extraordinary situation I just didn't know how to correct or get out of. Now, years later, I believe he would have eventually calmed down and become more of a family man simply because most of us do change and mature and evolve with age. He also saw and lived the devotion his father had for his mother—in this sense, I believe he had a good model to follow, despite the difficult circumstances of their lives. With his mom, Sal acted out the "prince of the family" role. Together they were funny: he swaggered and she responded softly but with a force. I enjoyed watching him with his grandmothers, who were both so in love with him, and he with them. He treated them with an air of reverence: they were sacred to him and in the dynamic between them he let himself go completely.

Very often, in order to liberate myself and my mind from him and his life, I went to Italy—sometimes even two or three times a year. I started to look out beyond the horizon of my life with him, though I wasn't really aware of this at the time. Not that I didn't want him—I did. But I loved going to Italy and wanted to live something that was just for me, that he wouldn't be a part of—just as he did. I guess, in retrospect, it was my way of saving something of myself for myself, because he really had worn me down. He didn't understand my ties to Italy and I wasn't interested in letting him in on any of that. It was sort of like "Okay, we'll stay together and you'll have your thing and I'll have mine." In those days, even then, Italy wasn't just vacation—it was *life* for me and he knew he couldn't touch it. Then, as now, Italy was never negotiable.

Friends used to say to me, "You make him think he's too important. Hold back, don't give so much of yourself to him, don't show him how much you love him." Well, that advice, good or bad as it may have been, was worthless because he *was* that important. I loved giving myself to him without limit and showing him how much I loved him—but Italy was my refuge when I needed to step back and regroup. I went every chance I got. Sal sent me off grudgingly, but always gave me money to put in my shoe and got sad and clingy at the airport. He always hugged and kissed me hard and tight before I had to board, never wanting to let go.

Before departing, I always had to leave an itinerary with both Sal and my mother so that they would know where I was to be found on any given day. Very early one Sunday morning when we were twenty-two, I was staying in a little hotel room on the beach right below Taormina, Sicily, with my old friend Jane. The phone on my nightstand rang. It was Sal, who asked me how everything was. "Salvie," I said, "we must come here to Sicily together. It is beyond description. The sea, the mountains, the intensity of the sun's light, the people, the color, the music, the food. You would love it here."

"And what are you going to do today?"

"I don't know. We'll probably go to the beach."

"My dad wants you to go see Cousin Turiddu in Calatabiano, our town." He passed the phone to his dad, who told me how to get there. So Jane and I flew out of bed, showered, had a coffee and got on our way in our little rented Fiat.

Taormina is a beautiful town on a mountain high above the sea filled with palm trees and bougainvillea and wild orchids that caters to people with sophisticated tastes. Driving inland brought us into another world. The landscape eventually became very dry, arid, and unwelcoming and Etna loomed large over us at all times. On we went, with Jane driving and me navigating. After a while we found the right turn onto the country road we had to follow—it was straight and narrow and went for quite a few kilometers until we suddenly found ourselves in the main piazza of Calatabiano.

We stopped the car and saw no fewer than two hundred men, only men, dressed in black, some in jackets, some in vests and black pants, all wearing little black caps or fedoras—all just standing around in the piazza. There we were, two totally stupid twenty-two-year-old American girls dressed in shorts and tank tops. I looked at her and said, "Jane, we are not getting out of this car." They were all staring right at us and we stared back, wondering if it was possible to just turn the car around and leave. It was all so very uncomfortable.

Suddenly a young man appeared at Jane's window and said in English, "Who are you?'

'We are here to find the family of some friends of ours. We are looking for Turiddu Fichera. We are from America—we are friends of Turiddu's cousin Filippo Testa."

The boy went and spoke with a few of the men dressed in black, who were all still staring at us, and came back and said, "I think I know where you want to go. You follow me in my car.'

Jane said to me, "Are we sure we want to do this?'

"Absolutely, he's in his car, we're in ours, all is fine. No worries." And off we went through the minuscule streets of this little town that time forgot and Jesus never visited, until we came to a little street. He stopped and indicated that we should too, then went into a little house there. After a few moments he came back out and said, "I think I have found the house where you want to go." We thanked him profusely and off he went. We never even got his name, sadly, nor did we ever see him again.

— We went into this tiny house where there lived an old man and his old wife. Their living room was their dining room was their kitchen, with a fireplace in the corner. They were so warm, so welcoming and sweet, quickly offering us coffee and home-baked cookies and their entire home. I was moved by their effusive warmth. After a few moments, I said in Italian, "I am a friend of Alfia and Philip Testa of America and they told me to visit you today and bring you their greetings."

"AAAAAAA ALFIA E FILIPPO. CHE BELLI!"

I thought, *Oh, thank God, we're okay here.* After a while, the man went into a back room and got some photos and put them in front of me. He said, "Vedi, questi sono Alfia e Filippo." It was a photo of a beautiful bride and groom, but they were not the Alfia and Philip that I knew. I stared at the photo for a long time thinking, *Oh my God, we've wound up in the wrong house and they've given us their coffee, their cookies, and their warm and loving hospitality. How the hell do I get out of this now?*

I looked at the man and said, "No, no, scusatemi, pero..." *Excuse me, but this isn't the Alfia and Philip I know. I don't know who these people are.* He jabbed his index finger onto the photo again and again and shouted, "Si si si, questi sono Alfia e Filippo d'America!'

The wife chimed in, yelling at him, and I just continued to insist that the lovely couple in the photo was not the couple I knew in Philadelphia until, totally exasperated, the old man went once again into the back room and came back out with more photos. As I started to go through them, I realized that something very wonderful had just happened: all of a sudden, in front of me were the wedding pictures of Mr. T's little sister Mary. I recognized all the faces in the photo: Uncle Pete, Uncle John, Aunt Millie, Aunt Connie, Aunt Antoinette, Mr. T, the bride Mary, and the groom, John Masi. I was so relieved to realize that I was actually in the "right" home.

Only then did I ask the old man his name. I said to him in Italian, "I am looking for Turiddu. Is that you?"

"No, I am Ignazio, but I will take you to him."

We all got back in the car, the old man and his wife coming with us. Jane drove through the little streets with the old man telling her to drive slowly, because you never know when a herd of sheep or cattle will come round a corner. We found ourselves at another house. The old man got out and went to the door and knocked and spoke and before we knew it there was a crowd of people around us—the welcoming committee, if you will, leading us into the house: the home, finally, of Turiddu, his wife Concettina, and their three beautiful daughters. They enveloped us in their warmth, their love, their welcome, and we immediately felt totally and completely at home. It was as though we had known them forever. Ignazio and his wife stayed.

Before we knew it half the town had arrived with coffee and cannoli and pastries and it had become a party. They were all so beautiful in their modest but extremely dignified home. I was in heaven, but also in difficulty trying to answer all of their questions about Alfia and Filippo. There was a lot of confusion and activity and chatter. The three daughters clung to Jane and me—they wanted to know about America and be close to us. They were gorgeous and smart and clearly had more to offer the world than that little town would have allowed.

After a while, I needed to go to the bathroom. I asked Concettina, "Dov'é il bakaus?" and she didn't understand me.

'Ma che cosé il *bakaus*?" What is the *bakaus*?

Now you must know that all my life, my grandfather, Giovanni "John" Bonavita, called the bathroom the *bakaus* and I believed that the word for bathroom in Italian was *bakaus*—but they had no idea at all what the hell I was talking about. I went off on my own until I found the bathroom, but they still didn't understand me. When I got home, Sal met me at the airport and we went straight into his house so that I could recount the whole story to Mr. T, who savored every single morsel. When I came to *bakaus* he looked at me with his eyes wide. Laughing, he said, "Did you really ask them where the *bakaus* was?"

"Yes, of course, I had to go!"

He started to laugh and laugh. "Don't you know that *bakaus* is an English word? In the old days the toilets were in the back of the house. With their Italian accents, *back house* became *bakaus*." For years he never let go of that story.

TWENTY-TWO

IN EARLY 2013, I finally mustered the courage to read Philip Leonetti's book *Mafia Prince*. It was a gut-wrenching experience for me because he reveals so much about how deeply immersed in it all Sal actually was. I felt strangely disconnected from many of these details, although I remember each story quite well. It felt as though I was reading fiction or a factual book about people I didn't know or have never met.

Philip was one of Sal's closest friends and the nephew of Mr. Scarfo. They were both convicted in federal court, along with a group of others, for Salvatore's murder and various other crimes. Sal considered Philip a brother.

Of course I knew Philip, too. I knew him well. He was one of the people who turned on Scarfo after they were all arrested and charged. Apparently those who turned (and there were quite a few) did so because they no longer wished to live under Scarfo's tactics of fear and intimidation. Sal's murder apparently was the drop that broke the vase, so to speak: he was extremely loyal and a good earner and many of them felt that if Salvie wasn't safe, then no one was. They were obviously not wrong.

Philip's mother was Scarfo's sister. They lived in Atlantic City, in what was once a vibrant and thriving Italian community called Ducktown. My mother used to call that neighborhood "the garlic belt" because at any time of the day or night, going through it, the fragrance of garlic frying in oil permeated the air. Philip's father disappeared when he was still quite young, so his uncle raised him as his own. All he knew was that life, which makes his redemption that much more poignant and nearly impossible to fathom and comprehend. I found his book amazing because it displays him as a profound man—something I never saw in him because the shadow he lived in was large and thick. Additionally, although I am not one to praise anyone who turns on his friends, in this case I must commend Philip for his courage; I admire his strength in transforming and redeeming himself, as I am certain he suffered greatly before moving toward the light. The truth is that, in that world, no one has "friends"; there are no friends. There are only "associates." Anyone can turn on anyone else at any time. Sal's murder proved the truth of that; that's why those who turned did so. That's why they were all caught and tried in two courts of law and why they ultimately answered to justice. Those who turned may have been trying to save themselves from decades-long prison terms, but Sal proved himself and his worth—as a true "friend" and in his, shall we say, "professional capacity"—time and time again. They knew who he was and the reasons for, and significance of, killing him. Philip, more than anyone in these stories, is the ultimate Shakespearean tragic hero, who pays dearly for his own actions and then spends his life trying to understand and accept the ramifications.

One time, when we were in Atlantic City, Sal said, "Let's stop and see Nicky." I said okay and off we went. There on Georgia Avenue the houses are old and large and very close together. His wife Mimi let us in and accompanied us into the dining room. She had fuzzy blond hair, blue eyes, and a tiny face and was timid and shy but very sweet. The entryway of the house was quite dark and the air heavy. The dining-room walls were covered in ordinary plywood paneling. In each of the room's four corners stood a coat of armor. When I whispered to Sal "This is too fucking weird and I want to leave," he pointed his index finger at me and told me to try to behave myself. I'd never seen such a badly decorated room before, nor had I ever felt the dark, heavy energy I felt in that house. It felt like a crowded South Broad Street funeral home on the night of a viewing.

Mr. Scarfo greeted me warmly, with a kiss on each cheek, then sat down and directed his attention to Sal. They spoke softly. After a few minutes he rang a little dinner bell and Mimi came running in. He asked her to make some coffee, then looked at me and said, "Why don't you go in the kitchen with Mimi and help her?" Sal shot me a quick look as if to say *Don't even question it.*

So into the kitchen I went with Mimi. She was from the small town in Calabria where Nicky's parents were born. After his first wife left him, he went there to find another wife and met Mimi. I had known his first wife, Theresa, who left him. She threatened, "If you don't divorce me, I'm going to stand in the middle of Ninth and Christian and scream about how much I hate you all day and all night." He let her go. With the kid. Unheard of. Theresa became a manicurist in a fancy salon on the Main Line outside of Philadelphia—she was attractive and slightly nuts, but I always admired her courage and she had it to give away.

Then he found little Mimi in Calabria, waiting for her big break to come to America. All I could think about was, *Does she like her life? Is she happy with this man? Does she really think she's better off here than in some poor little village in southern Italy?* She was very sweet, shy but open at the same time—as though she wanted someone to talk to. I sensed a heaviness around her, a sorrow, and was certain it wasn't my imagination. As far as the big picture, well, I was so amazed by this whole reality that I couldn't wait to be gone. And, very quickly, we were.

When we were safely in the car, I told Sal that being in that house had been the single strangest experience I'd ever had in my life. I told him of my impressions about the thickness of the air and Mimi's resignation and, of course, he got upset with me. Sal considered Mr. Scarfo a second father; he loved him. The feeling may have been reciprocated, actually, before things turned, but I've no way of knowing for sure.

I saw Mr. Scarfo many times after that. I saw him for the last time that day in court, when Sal's sister testified for the prosecution. That was in 1987 or '88—I no longer remember.

TWENTY-THREE

S AL'S MOTHER ALFIA WAS tall and blond, with deep-set eyes, blue as the Aegean. She had the most classical bone structure of anyone I've ever known—a Roman, aquiline nose; high, chiseled cheekbones and a strongly angled jaw. She had beautiful, broad, square shoulders but was very slim—she cared for herself and paid attention—and had long, beautiful hands graced only by a very thick gold wedding band and an antique gold watch that was actually one link after another of gold bows. Sounds awful, but you just had to see it. It was beautiful, her watch. Classic and unique, as she was. I loved her with all my heart and still do.

"So what are you gonna do? Are you gonna marry him?" she asked me as she poured coffee for both of us one day in her kitchen.

"I don't know, Mrs. T. I love him—you know—he's my best friend, we share everything, we do everything together—but I'm a little afraid. I'm a little scared. What kind of life will I have? What could happen?"

This was *long* before anyone had been murdered in the street and exposed for all to see, before any of us had any fear about what the future might hold and what horrors had yet to unfold, but still I was apprehensive.

She said, "Look at me. Look at how I live. Look at my life. This would all be yours. I love him more than anything in the world. He's my son. But I love you, too. You're only twenty-three years old. You need to know. You don't come from this world. I didn't come from this world. My people were farmers down in Jersey—they sent me to live on Ninth and Christian with my grandparents so I could go to school and then I met him, I met my husband. We were kids. He was very persistent, like Sal is with you, and I didn't know what to

75

make of all of it. He was very charming, you know, flirty. And I fell. And then it was done. And now this is my life and it's very hard. Do you know how many times I've made dinner, working all day in the kitchen, and he would come downstairs all dressed up in a black silk suit and say, 'Oh, I'm sorry, I won't be here for dinner tonight, I've got something to do' and I'd be left alone with the kids? Why, even when Maria was born, he was away. I delivered her on my own with my family around me. It's not easy, you know. It hurts. How many times have I made dinner only to have no one come home to eat it? No phone calls, no explanations. And you can't ask any questions. It's the life. This would be your life; this would be what you have to take. You have to believe and know you can do it and it's not easy, no matter how much you think you love him."

I didn't have any answers for her in that moment, but I knew it would never be for me. When you joined that world, your life was closed off into a self-contained bubble of excuses, explanations, and extrapolations of reality—because how else could you live? You couldn't be conspicuous as a wife or as a woman in that world, you couldn't be noticed, you couldn't really have much of a life at all outside of your home—if, that is, you were going to live the life correctly. Mostly the wives only associated with each other, and I didn't really fit in well with many of them. They were mostly either very sweet, quiet, demure, and religious or cold, calculating, sneaky, and vicious. This is how I saw most of the wives; ultimately, each of the women I knew well just had to figure out a way to survive and take care of her family in an extremely unsettling and difficult situation. It was all about survival. I saw myself nowhere in this scheme.

I lived large, spiritually and emotionally, and I loved to work and have thousands of friends and a full, rich, open life. But I also knew that to be together, to stay together, Sal needed me to bring everything in my life down to a much smaller and more manageable level. Even now, I am so deeply grateful that his mom spoke with me so frankly about things that had, until that point, always remained unstated between him and me. I know she loved me, as I loved her, but I think she really just wanted her son to be happy with the right person and she wasn't so sure that that person was me. I think, too, that she saw a little bit of herself in me—a young woman torn between her own world, her own family culture, and her love for a man from a different cultural situation in which she could not really imagine herself.

Mrs. T's parents, Leonardo and Rosaria Arciadiacono, lived in a small ranch house in Swedesboro, New Jersey, near the farm they owned and tended. She worked on the farm with them when she was a young girl and helped her mother raise her three younger brothers. When they retired, Mr. T, Sal's dad, bought them their little ranch house. I used to love to go down there to visit them and Uncle Joe, Mrs. T's youngest brother, who still lived with his parents and looked after them for her. Sal was very devoted to his grandparents—we used to go down there once a week for years and visit and have dinner or lunch on a Saturday afternoon.

Little Grandmom, as I called her, was short and round and completely, totally, madly in love with her grandson. He, too, loved her madly and would hug her and kiss her forehead and do Muhammad Ali pretend punches to tease her; she'd look at me and say "Rosa, what the hell's wrong with him?" Grandmom sang when she spoke, and nothing was more beautiful than the smile on her face as she stood at the door watching us pull up in the car. She was a great cook—when she knew Sal was coming she'd make a feast and we'd all sit at the kitchen table together (with the TV on, because Grandpop wanted to watch the news).

They were born in Sicily, in Giarre, a hardscrabble little town just a few minutes inland from Taormina. You knew from their skin that they were Sicilian because they tanned golden brown with just a tinge of red. Neither of them had wrinkles. They both had light eyes and, although their hair was already white when I knew them, they had once been more blond than dark. Grandpop and Joe used to make good homemade wine—not at all tart or bitter—which we'd drink with every meal.

Sal loved his grandfather too. Grandpop had worked so hard at farming for so long that his hip bones were basically gone—he couldn't take one step without his walker or crutches. He was a big, sturdy bull of a man but the arthritis got the best of him. He was always in pain and somewhat sad but so very sweet. Sal would hug him and kiss him and say things like, "Hey Pop, whaddya say we unload Grandmom and go find some babes, me and you?" He enjoyed making Grandpop laugh and always joked with him. There was always a palpable love and sweetness and gentility in that house. I loved being there with them. Mr. T essentially supported them; they loved him, but they were afraid of the life. Grandmom used to tell Sal to go to school and study and forget the streets. He would just tease her in response and say he was going to be the next Muhammad Ali.

When Grandpop's health started to fail, Mrs. T went back and forth between Swedesboro and South Philadelphia every day (one hour each way) to look after him and help Grandmom. She and Joe lifted and bathed and dressed him. Very hard work, but she never, ever, ever complained. One day, an old friend of hers who had a completely different spirit said to her, "Oh, Al, these old people are gonna be the death of us." Mrs. T was appalled. She replied, "If I had to, I would take care of my parents for a hundred years and be grateful that I still had them with me."

Grandpop eventually died in late 1978 and, not even two months later, Mrs. T was diagnosed with cancer—multiple myeloma—in her spine. She died just eighteen months later, on November 5, 1980. While she lived she was at the service of everyone around her. She did everything for everyone every day—cook, clean, wash, and iron—in her own home and her parents'. She walked to church every morning for the 8:30 mass and was particularly devoted to St. Jude, the patron saint of hopeless cases. Afterward she'd come to my house and have coffee with my mother. She loved my mother's irreverence, her crazy say-anything-in-front-of-anyone brand of wildness, and my mother, to make her laugh and enjoy herself even more, purposely always laid it on thick. My mother loved her deeply and their friendship was very important to her.

When Mrs. T became sick and became weak, my mother was in that house every day helping her, along with Mrs. T's two best friends from the old neighborhood, Theresa and Emma. Mr. T would talk to my mother and the other ladies in private about his worries, about how sick his wife was, about how he didn't know what to do, where to go, how to help her, and asked for their help. My mother and the ladies always told him that they'd always be there to do anything and everything possible to make her comfortable and to look after her. That was actually when I got to know that other side of Mr. T—the exceptionally devoted husband—and I saw a dimension to his soul that I had never seen before. As she became sicker, he had a look of fear and sadness on his face that never left, only deepened. I think he was so filled with fear by the thought of losing her that he began to mourn her even before she passed. In the last month before she passed, he almost never moved from his spot by her bed. I would go in and upstairs to visit with her and he'd be reading to her from a book or magazine or watching television. I'd sit there and hang out and we'd read her St. Jude prayers together. In front of me he made his mood light and teasing, but his eyes—the sadness in them was quite profound. His eyes were always wet even if I never saw him cry. One time Mrs. T joked, "Oh yeah, pretty soon you'll be out at the nightclubs looking for somebody new and young." He replied (not at all in a maudlin way), "Alfia, I thank God every day that you are my wife and that you will always be my wife." She looked at me and said, "See, there's nothing I can do." Their love was huge and full and playful and so very genuine.

We watched her slip away inch by inch and, quite frankly, nothing was more awful for Salvatore. Mother and son worshipped each other. She was nothing if not the classic loving Italian mother whose son was her hero. It drove him crazy that she was dying and he could do nothing to halt this process, but he was in total denial. He never wanted to discuss her illness with me, despite my efforts to get him to open up about his feelings.

We were just twenty-four when she died. Then and only then, in the aftermath, did he begin to speak about what he felt about losing her. He was hugely embarrassed to cry in front of me so, as he spoke, sometimes I would look away from him to help him preserve his pride. It was very hard for him to open himself up to his emotions and express them freely, but sometimes I would just force him to—and this was one of those times. It was difficult, too, for him to fully express his feelings for his mother, especially with my family and me, since we too were all mourning her loss, but suffice it to say that he loved her deeply and never did recover from losing her.

It is not an exaggeration to say that Salvie and I "raised" each other—we really did. We taught each other everything: on an emotional level, on a sexual level, on an intellectual level. All by ourselves. We were practically babies when we met and then, through the years, we helped each other through life events that simply do not usually occur to people our age. We never left each other—even when we weren't together for those two years before he died, we sometimes spoke by phone. We were honest about our feelings: that we missed each other and that we always thought of each other and looked for each other and needed each other. We raised each other and helped each other through every single thing we had to live and go through, but it truly was far too much for us to handle with great maturity, kids that we were. I think that now I understand just about everything that we lived through together—and I know, too, that before he died he came to understand what was important.

When Mrs. T died, the funeral home ran out of cars for the flowers—they had to call them in from all of the other funeral homes in South Philadelphia. There was the hearse, then Mr. T's car, and nineteen more open cars filled with flowers. When Mr. T. realized this, he instructed the funeral director to allow only one car to travel in the procession to the cemetery. He sent all of the other cars to every church in South Philadelphia to place the flowers on their altars.

After she passed, there was no one sadder in the world than him. Sal always pretended he was okay, but Mr. T never bothered to perform or show himself as anything but what he was: completely bereft with grief. That's when Sal and I began to think seriously about getting married, and I was frightened to the core of the whole idea. The love, the connection, the closeness were all still there. The collective mourning was very deep and very big—and then it was just him and his dad in that house and me in mine, and so it was only logical to begin to speak of us and our future. But how do you build a happy and healthy future on so much pain and sadness and uncertainty? How could I feel joyful building that future, knowing that my life would become enveloped by that house and that life three doors away? I saw that I would slowly become a prisoner. I could see myself doing nothing but washing and cooking and maybe later dealing with kids and all their stuff. Little by little, inch by inch, my world—which I needed to be large and full—would shrink and shrink and shrink down to God knows what.

Losing his mom, I have come to believe, was the real beginning of the end. It might seem logical to think that the beginning of the end for Sal was actually in March 1980, when his godfather Angelo Bruno was killed, shot dead while exiting his car in front of his house late one night. Really, though, it was Sal's mother's death, because that was when he began to go inside of himself and very, very slowly become impenetrable. That was the beginning of his great transformation.

I never questioned my love. Every cell of my body loved him and accepted all the hurt and betrayal. I loved his dad, too, who was always nothing but loving and sweet and very playful with me. I wanted to be there to help them, but I didn't want to lose my life. I have never, before or since, been so torn in two—and I didn't know how to even say the first word about any of it to him because I was so deathly afraid of hurting him more. He and his dad wore their mourning, literally, in the form of black armbands. All the time. They were always together in those months after she passed—Sal never ever left his father's side. I wanted to try to help them through and make them happy but I feared losing myself in the process, and I know now that I would have. I would have done anything to help lift that thick black veil from their lives, but I knew I would not have been capable. Maybe never.

That December, I lost my Uncle Frank, one of my life's great teachers and heroes, and my heart sank further down. Neither of us could help the other then, and we went into a dark period. Everyone tried to elevate our moods, our hearts, but there really wasn't anything to do. That Christmas there were no wreaths, no lights, no trees, not in my house and not in his.

Little by little by little, we began to come out of it. We would still hang out and make love in his room and talk and laugh and watch TV and sing along to Marvin Gaye.

And then it was March. This was 1981. On the evening of the fourteenth—it was a Saturday—Sal said, "Do you want to have dinner tonight at the restaurant with my father?" I said yes, so we went around six-thirty or seven to sit with his dad and have a meal. They still had their black armbands on. Dad was sweet, as always.

We began to tell him about a wedding we had been to the week before—a wedding in which I was a bridesmaid—and he looked at us, put his fork down, and said, "And when are you two going to make me a grandfather? Mom's gone, your sister's doing God knows what in New York, you two are here. When are you going to make me a grandfather?"

We looked at each other, Sal and me, and smiled and shook our heads up and down as if we were saying "yes." We turned to him and said, "Soon. Promise. Soon." Then we finished up our dinners, stayed a little longer talking with some friends at the bar, and went home. We didn't talk about Dad's comment on the way home—or ever again, until three and a half years later—on the last night we had together. Instead we made love with Marvin Gaye in the background, as we always did, and fell asleep for a little while.

Around one o'clock Sal said, "I have to go back to the restaurant. He's waiting for me. I'll have a shower and then I'll walk you home and go." And that's what we did. I got into my bed that night around one-thirty and went to sleep fast.

At three-fifteen, I felt a huge rush of air come from the front of the house. I heard an explosion and then the sound of all the glass in my mother's room breaking and her screaming. It seemed to be in slow motion, but it all happened in a fraction of a second. I was up on my feet and wide awake in that same fraction of a second, running down the hallway. I bumped into my father, who was running toward my mother's room, then ran down the stairs and out the door and looked to the right, toward the old ARCO refineries, which I thought had exploded. In the sky on the right, I saw nothing. I was overwhelmed by the stench of sulfur—of rotten eggs.

And then I looked to the left and saw smoke hanging in the air. The front porch of Sal's house looked all splintered and fragmented and broken. There was complete silence. I ran down my steps and over to his house, which was completely blown apart, and couldn't even see that someone was lying on the ground just inside the house, right there at the front door. As I stood frozen at the bottom of his front steps, not knowing if I should go up and into the house, I felt hands on my shoulders pulling me away, back toward my house. It was my dad right behind me. He ran right up onto the porch and into the doorway.

I was screaming, "Dad, Dad, is it Sal? Daddy, is it Sal?"

"I don't know who it is. Go home now and try and call Sal." My dad remained there with Mr. T, who was unconscious.

Sal answered the phone.

"Salvie, is your dad with you?"

"No, no he's not. Why are you asking me that? WHY ARE YOU ASKING ME THAT?" He started yelling.

"Sal, there was just an explosion in your house."

The line went down.

The cops arrived and cordoned off the house. They realized immediately that Mr. T was still alive. Thank God he didn't have to die right there, to be left there for hours, gawked at and photographed. He was still alive, so they were forced to take him to Saint Agnes's ER. I was outside—in my red flannel pajamas the whole time. By then a huge crowd had gathered. Suddenly I heard people yelling: "Here comes Sal, here comes Sal!"

I saw him running through the park and tried to intercede, to grab him, but he was wild; he was out of his mind, screaming, "Where's my father? This is my house! All of you get the fuck out of here!"

Sal's best friend Joseph, who was across the street, grabbed him and tried to pull him off the scene, but there was no containing him. We dragged him into a car and sped off to the hospital, where we waited. It felt like forever, but it was only seventy-five minutes after the bomb went off when the doctors came out to Sal and said they were so very sorry.

Then I saw a Salvatore I had never seen before. He went into a small room there in the ER and slammed the door shut, and all I heard was breaking—he shattered every glass cabinet, vial, medicine bottle, and piece of equipment in that room. I heard sounds come from him that didn't sound human. He was crying, screaming, and roaring—he was actually roaring. There was nothing to do. Nothing. The few of us waiting in the hallway were speechless, just looking back and forth at each other wordlessly. I tried to get near him but he didn't see me or hear me. It was as though he was gone and some other force had taken over. Aunt Antoinette, everyone's favorite and the stable rock of the Testa family, was also there that night. I knew that she was the only person who could handle him in this state. I suddenly felt so useless—nothing and no one could have helped him in that moment. He didn't even see me standing in front of him, he was so outside of himself. After a while, Aunt Annie took hold of him and took him to her house, and one of the guys took me home. When I arrived I discovered that my dad had taken my mother to the hospital, too, since the glass of her bedroom windows had broken all over her—and she'd had a heart attack from fright.

The priests at our parish church, Saint Monica, didn't want to give Mr. T a mass of Christian burial. I remember Sal saying to his sister, "Fuck them. Fuck those motherfuckers. Who needs them?"

His sister replied, "Sal, we have to go and make nice because if they don't accept him into church for a mass, we won't be able to bury him with Mommy."

Sal, humbled by that thought, said, "Okay. You go talk. I don't want anything to do with them. Just ask them how fuckin" much they want. Motherfuckers."

Philip had his mass of Christian burial and was laid to rest right next to his beloved wife only four months after she departed.

The aftermath of that death is all a big, unfocused blur in my memory now—it's as though the screen went black and then stayed black for an entire year. Just black.

TWENTY-FOUR

ON MARCH 15, 1982, exactly one year to the day after his father's death, the lead story on the evening news was that a certain young man been found dead in a small parking lot in South Philadelphia with firecrackers and paper money stuffed into every orifice of his body.

This news made me sick and breathless.

"Sal, they say on the news that he's the guy who made and detonated the bomb that killed Dad. Sal, he wasn't my dad, but I loved him too so I understand this. I understand everything, Sal, and I will not, cannot, judge you. But please, please say you had nothing to do with this. Please tell me that you're not looking to avenge his loss. Please."

He just stared at me silently for a long time and then finally said, "You know I'm never going to say anything about any of this, right? I'm never going to answer any questions you have."

"Sal, do you realize the gravity of the danger you're putting yourself in? Do you realize that if you go down this road, you take me with you—you put me in danger, too? And what about our kids, Sal—the kids we want someday, the kids we've already named? Please stop and think for one moment about the kind of karma you are creating for yourself. Do you realize what this means for your life, for your future and for everyone in it?"

He just stared at me in silence.

All I wanted to do was be there for him and make him happy, help him put things back together so that he could move on. But all around us there was insanity. Every week, there was another killing, another murder out in the open light of day, someone else we knew well whose mother had to bury him. Madness. Utter and complete madness.

That was when I started to become really forceful with him about our need to get out. I wanted to get the fuck out of Philadelphia and leave all of these crazy people and Porter Street with all the gawking neighbors who knew far too much about us. I started lobbying really hard—and then our arguments got bad.

"You understand nothing," he would say to me. "After all these years, how can you understand nothing? I can't go anywhere. I have to stay right where I am. Right here. I'm a part of this thing. It's not a job you apply for, get, and then quit one day. It's for life. I can't go anywhere. You go where you want to go, but I have to stay right here and live what I live. You choose."

I pleaded with him to try to negotiate with whomever he had to—to let him go, to let him leave. To let him start somewhere else, far, far away from this world, now that his father was gone.

"Your position has changed. Nothing is what it once was. Let it go, Sal," I would say. "Let it go and let's go and give your life a chance to be something else. Let's give us a chance to be something else. We want horses and a ranch and a lot of kids. Let's go do it. But not here. We'll never ever do that here. I can't bring kids into this world because I know that someday you'll either be dead or in a federal prison somewhere, and then what? Then what? Do I bring your children to see you once a month for a two-hour visit to get to know you? Is that how you want to raise your children? Suppose you wind up in jail for a long time. What happens then? You'll change, Sal, you'll become someone else and maybe I will too, and then what happens to us? And what about if you die, God forbid it a million times? What happens to us? I'll work—I've always worked—but what about your kids? Who takes care of them? Just me alone? Sal, we have to think about these things."

He said once, "I can't believe how much you've changed since my father died." I replied, "And I can't believe how little you have. Haven't you learned anything from this? You cannot trust these people you've aligned yourself with, Sal, don't you see how crazy they are?

How sick they are? These people don't belong in and never were in your father or Godfather's class, Salvatore, don't you see that?"

He didn't understand me at all, didn't at all see what I saw, and on some level, in all of that confusion, I was slowly becoming the enemy; suddenly, there was this small gap in our individual views of the situation and the more we kept talking about it all, the larger that gap became.

During these arguments and discussions, we would just stare at each other, trying to find the bridge on which we could meet. We had never disagreed about anything this serious before. We fought all the time, with only a few tense moments of truce in between conversations. I feared for him and I feared for me and I feared for any children we might have someday. I fought him for all of us. And then I just got tired. I knew I was right and I knew that I knew the way out, but he wouldn't follow me down that road—and all I could think was that it was time. I was sure that I wouldn't or couldn't take one step toward him. I needed for him to cross that bridge entirely and come across to my way of thinking. Slowly, I began to understand how impossible this was for him.

It was time for me to start to make a break, because it wasn't going to change. Even with all the pain, the incalculable loss and horror, part of him still wanted that life and I, more and more, wanted nothing to do with it. But despite all of that, my love for him, what I felt for him, never diminished. I still loved him with all my heart, even though that little voice in my heart kept saying, over and over, *No no no no—it's time to make a break.*

When Sal died, I remember thinking that the time between his father's death in March of 1981 and the day Sal actually died was my period of mourning for him. I truly mourned his loss before he died because I knew, I really knew, what was coming and believed that it was only a matter of time.

TWENTY-FIVE

UDDENLY, IN THE SUMMER of 1982, the break I needed got made for me. Sal was in front of his hangout at Ninth and Christian, eating clams from a bucket and hanging out with a couple of buddies, when a car went by and two shooters shot him multiple times, almost cutting him in half at his abdomen.

He didn't die. He was in surgery for about a thousand hours—they were working hard to put him back together, literally. I went up to the hospital and just waited outside of surgery. I no longer remember who else was there although I am certain Aunt Antoinette, at least, was there. I was in another fucking world, just sitting there with no energy left in my body, wondering if he was dying in that operating room. Finally a doctor came out and said, "Well, he's alive, but it's really touch and go. But he's alive."

All I wanted to do was crawl on my knees to him, thanking God that he hadn't died at twenty-six. I wanted to see him so badly, but the doctor said, "No, that's not possible now. He's really, really in bad shape. I'm afraid you'll have to wait." So I waited. I slept in the waiting room that night, just waiting for an opportunity to go in and see him. Early the next morning it came. They were changing shifts or something like that and I saw the moment arrive. I just went through the doors into that intensive-care post-op recovery room and walked through it until I found him. It was like a scene from a movie, exaggerated and over the top—he was surrounded by all sorts of beeping machines and covered in bandages and tape, tubes and needles in his arms, but his eyes were open.

"Sal, Sal, I'm here. I'll always be here. I love you, Salvie. I love you and I'll never leave you."

His eyes moved—his eyes and his eyebrows—but of course he couldn't speak or respond in any way. I saw he was agitated. I told him to stay calm, that I was there, and I kissed him and left. I didn't know it then, but it would be two weeks before I saw him again. Had I known that, I would have never left that waiting room. That waiting room was where I left my heart.

TWENTY-SIX

S AL REMAINED IN INTENSIVE care for a while. I stayed away because his sister was very angry that I, that first morning, had been there and got in to see him. She said that my presence could have upset him greatly; he needed to rest and, most importantly, that "only family" should be present in any case. "Only family." It took a while for those words to sink through my skull. The way I coped with this nastiness was to recoil and withdraw and disappear and I did just that for two weeks.

When I returned to the hospital I found a situation I didn't recognize at all. Sal's sister was there, pregnant with her first child, sitting by his bed, keeping him company. I could not have been met with more coldness or less welcome if I had been one of the shooters myself. I tried to ignore it and tried to start a conversation, but Sal didn't even want to look at me. Honestly, both of them received me with such iciness that even thinking about it today, I still get that same heavy pain deep in my stomach. I had no idea what I had done. The walls around them felt impenetrable to me and I felt a despair that had no end.

I was also pregnant then. About three weeks. I had just found out a few days earlier, but there was no way I could have told him. Now, considering the impenetrable wall of ice in front of me, I was sure I couldn't tell him. So I kept it to myself while trying to sort out what I would do.

I went back a few more times but they literally would not speak to me or even look my way. They would only speak to each other in my presence about the constant and continuing visits of the young woman to whom he would eventually become engaged. I prefer not to remember her name, let alone share it with you. I just felt more and more as though they were circling the wagons and I was no longer considered a member of their select group. With each successive visit, that feeling only grew. My despair and sadness were overwhelming. And then the day came when I arrived at the hospital at six o'clock one morning and was met at the door by my doctor. I had already been up all night crying because of what I was about to do. He met me at the door of my car (my doctor was an angel), put his arm around my shoulder and let me cry into his neck. He said, "Don't you worry, you're doing what you feel is right and necessary at this moment of your life. I will take care of you as though you are my own child." I went into the hospital with him, the same hospital where Salvie was on another floor, and had an abortion. It was September 20, 1982. Two years later on that very same day, Sal would be laid to rest at Holy Cross Cemetery.

I think of that child every single day of my life and do not believe I will ever stop thinking of him. I sometimes speak to him, asking for his understanding and forgiveness.

After that day, I never attempted to contact Sal in any way again. I made every effort I felt I had to make to be okay, to heal myself, to move ahead with my life, and to help myself come through all the years of trauma and heartache.

TWENTY-SEVEN

1992 I now live in Italy, in Rome, fulfilling a lifetime dream. I work hard. I have a nice little apartment in Trastevere with a beautiful terrace filled with bougainvillea and am happy to be in the city and the country of my dreams. But it's hard. I am completely alone. I have friends, I have a job, I live in a home I love, but still and all I feel completely alone. I've started thinking almost constantly that I need to leave, to return home, and then it starts. Another recurring dream. I'm climbing up a mountain and there are big rocks under my feet, hampering my progress. Every once in a while I look up to see how far I have yet to go, and there is Sal. He is standing on top of the mountain, the sun behind him so he's in silhouette, and his arms are outstretched toward me. He's talking to me as I climb: "Come on. You can do this. I'm here. I'm right here. Don't worry about anything. I am here. Come on. Come on, you can do it." And I climb and climb and climb. Every single time, the dream is always the same.

TWENTY-EIGHT

OVER THE COURSE OF these past thirty years, I've replayed over and over in my head the most extraordinary event of my life.

It was August 1984, a hot, still, steamy night. I came home late from a dinner in Center City with friends. As I was parking my car, Sal suddenly pulled his car up next to mine and just stopped there and looked in at me. I froze. I didn't pull the window down or try to speak. We just stared at each other for a few moments until he rolled the window down and motioned for me to do the same.

I think I said, "What do you want?" Mind you, I hadn't seen him face-to-face like this in about two years.

"Can we talk, please?"

"No, Sal, I don't want to talk to you."

He did, as he had always done, the little motion of the head to the side and sad eyes. "Oh, please, RoRo, I need to talk to you."

I remember thinking, *When have you ever been able to say "No" to him? When?* "Okay," I said, "We can talk."

I got into his car. I was so nervous, excited, and even relieved to finally be near him and with him. Upon getting into the car, we hugged and kissed and then I felt it—I immediately sensed an awful aura, a thick air, around him—a heaviness that had an electrical charge to it. I know that it's easy to talk about in hindsight, but in that very moment, I shivered at the feeling I sensed. I knew he was in serious danger and had known that for several months; I knew that I too was placing myself in danger by sitting in that car in the middle of the street that hot, humid, quiet August night.

Although in two years I had "moved on," as we say now in 2014, sitting there and looking into his face and kissing each other in greeting made all that time and all that distance and all that work to overcome what I had endured just vanish. There we were, just us two kids, still—after all these years—so connected and intertwined with a deep, powerful, visceral bond and still crazy for each other. And then the conversation started.

"How you doing? What's new? Oh, you're back in school? Good for you, I'm proud of you. Oh, you work with people with AIDS? Be careful with that—that's a scary thing. Any boyfriends?"

He said that all was okay with him (of course I knew better) but that, since his mother was gone, his father was gone, his sister lived far away, and he was all alone (even if he wasn't, I believe he thought and felt that he was), his life had no meaning. "Rosina, I have nothing. I have nothing left. My life has no meaning and I don't care about anything but my little niece." He pulled out a photo of the eighteen-month-old girl named for his mother. "Look, look how beautiful she is. She's all I care about." Imagine that: he kept an eight-by-ten photo of her, sheathed in plastic, in the glove box of his car.

We talked about the article about him that had appeared in the *Wall Street Journal* that April. I said I absolutely hated it and he said he did too. "That's all I need," he said. "That's the kind of thing that gets you killed."

"Oh and by the way, congratulations on breaking that engagement, Sal, which just might have been the most insane thing you've ever done."

"You have no idea how insane that was." The young lady in question, he said, had told him all sorts of stories about me and my alleged infidelities, had essentially filled his head with all sorts of crazy lies and stories to drive a wedge between us. She had his phone number changed, he believed to prevent me from calling him, and had transformed his house into a place in which he no longer felt welcome and that he no longer recognized.

"What the fuck am I going to do with a Jacuzzi in my bathroom?" he asked. "Do you want to come inside and see it? See how ridiculous it is?"

I respectfully declined. He said that he had bought a new home at the shore. The title was to be in the names of his sister and her husband, not his; when the "fiancée" found out about it, she became enraged: "And what about me? What do I get if you get killed?"

That, he said, was really the final straw.

I said, "It's a very good thing you came out of that, Sal," but still I felt so afraid for him.

"Yeah, good thing I woke up from that bad dream and that it's all over."

I understood why he had done that—he was alone and he had never been so lonely, so beaten down and so vulnerable in his entire life.

It was crushing for us to contemplate how many people were against us. We were surrounded by people who never had our best interests in mind or heart at all. This was a very devastating thing for us to fathom, but we were able to discuss it all openly and with complete honesty that night. We talked a great deal about how the illness of envy is a far worse thing than hatred and how that envy had affected us individually and as a couple.

"If I give you the new number, will you call me?" Of course I said I would. As I reached for my little book in my bag, half under my breath, I said, "Let's see, do I write it under S for Sal or T for Testa?"

"How about under L for 'lifelong'?"

And that's what I did.

He said he had gone through all of his money and had almost nothing left. "They're all always asking me to lend them money and how can I say no? And then they never pay me back." That made me want to vomit because I knew what it meant. I knew that he did too, but was not prepared to acknowledge that truth consciously.

After a while, I began to feel afraid. There we were in the middle of the dark street, not a soul anywhere around us. I felt very exposed and vulnerable.

"Sal, park the car, please, and let's go and sit on my porch or on your porch—I don't want to sit in the car." I thought we would be less conspicuous up on the porch, so that was what we did. Years later I learned that he was already being stalked by his potential killers, who were waiting for the right moment to take him away.

We began to reminisce. We talked about meeting as kids on the boardwalk in Ventnor and how I thought he was a conceited little ass and he thought I was a pretty girl. We talked about going to the Spectrum to see the closed-circuit Muhammad Ali fights and going horseback riding down in Jersey. We talked about Apache, his horse, dying; we talked about my grandfather, who loved him and who died when we were nineteen. Until the end, Pop always called him "Mike," never Salvatore. That made us laugh.

We talked about all of his grandparents, two of whom had died at that point, and about his mother getting sick and what her dying did to him. We relived the day she died, which was huge for both of us. I had been the first person in the house after she passed early that morning, and I didn't leave until well into the next day. We talked about the death of his father, reliving the sequence of events that night, truly the worst thing to happen in his life, and how that had been the end of his world—and I knew it.

We talked about us as a couple, as two kids in love.

"I never loved anyone in my life as much as I loved you—besides my family, you are the best thing that ever came to me," he said. "You've always been there—through everything—my mother getting sick and then dying, what happened to my father, you were always there. I understand now what you meant all the times you used to say that you wished I only had two subway tokens in my pocket. I used to think you didn't want me to have good luck, but now I understand. I never felt used by you; I never felt like you wanted anything from me but to love you, and I did and still do. RoRo, it was really always you."

I knew this was all true. "So why did you lie and cheat and treat me so badly? How did we get here, Sal? How did we get to this point? I never loved anyone in my life the way I loved you either, but you weren't good to me in the right way. You pushed me away and away and away until this."

"Don't ask me any questions. Okay? Promise? Don't ask me what I'm talking about when I tell you something I need to tell you."

Rolling my eyes and feeling that same old exasperation, I said, "Oh, what the fuck. Whaaaaaat?"

'I owe you an apology. I have to say 'I'm sorry,' because only now do I wish I had listened to you all these years. You were right, you know, you were always right and I see it now, I know it now and I wish I had listened to you long ago." Naturally, I asked him what he was talking about.

"No questions. You were right about everything. You were always right about everything and everybody all along. Okay? That's all I'll say."

I did not feel victorious. I knew I was right and I knew what I felt in his presence—sorrow, desolation, resignation—looking at his destiny and thinking that just maybe it was not what he wanted but completely bereft of any idea how to change anything now.

And then he asked me: "Do you still love me?"

I stared at him silently for several moments and then replied, "Sal, I will love you for the rest of my life and into the next one and the one after that and the one after that."

After a few moments of silence, he asked me, "Do you think we'll ever get it together in this life and, you know, get married and have those kids we always wanted?"

Before answering, I thought, *Should I tell him? Should I tell him how insanely afraid I am for him and for his life and future now? Should I tell him what I truly feel in my heart or should I lie to him so he feels better? Can I even say out loud what I feel in my guts to be true?*

Crying almost uncontrollably now, I looked right at him and said, "No, Sal, I really don't. I don't think we'll ever manage to get it together in this life."

He looked at me and didn't say anything for what seemed to be a long while. We just kept looking at each other, not saying anything, both crying—me sobbing, him with just tears. Then he said something that was so not him, so not who he was, how he lived, what he thought, what he believed—something so out of line with his spirit, with his character.

"Well, that's okay. It's okay, Ro, because I'll be waiting for you. I'll be looking for you the next time around and we'll get it right then."

For a long time, then, we just sat in silence with my head on his shoulder and holding hands until, finally, dawn began to make herself seen and felt. I had to go to work, but there we still were out on that front porch and I didn't want to leave him. I wanted to stay with him forever. I wanted the night and day to last for a thousand years.

I no longer remember who said good night to whom first, but we stood up and we hugged and kissed and cried for a long time. I asked him to please be careful, to be safe and watchful. One of us said that we should have done that—should have talked so openly, only with our hearts—more often in the past. We both said "I love you" a hundred times, and then we separated and that was it.

All I did was cry for the next three weeks, morning, noon, and night. Day after day, at work, at home, on the subway, on the bus, walking the streets, always, always, always in tears, because this was a love far beyond anything I was able to manage. I kept asking God, "Why did you make this happen? Why did you make us see each other? What the fuck is wrong with you that you're always playing these horribly cruel jokes on me?"

And then I knew why. About three or so weeks after that night, on September 15, at six-thirty on a Saturday morning, I got word that Sal had been found dead. My very first thought upon hearing that news was to thank God for not having called my Salvatore home without first giving us the chance to see each other, speak about our love, and affirm that love for the last time in this life.

I have never, ever, ever stopped replaying the events of that night in my mind. For me, that night was miraculous.

TWENTY-NINE

*I*AM AT SAL'S HOUSE—NOT *the house I know, but it is his house—and there is a party. I am annoyed by the presence of all these people I don't know very well. He is dressed in a suit and happy by my side. He says, "How about if you call in sick from work the next two days and we hang out?"*

"But, Sal, I work for Ralphie now. I can't lie to my brother."

"Oh, come on. He would understand." Then he puts his head way down and to the side and lifts his eyes way up. "Oh please. Come on. What wouldn't you do to spend two more days with me?"

"Okay, let me get rid of all these people—let me clear out the house and get rid of everybody and I will be right back. Don't go anywhere, I'll be back real soon."

I awaken feeling frustrated because he hasn't come back and I can't reach him to find out when he is coming back.

THIRTY

I WAS SLEEPING IN MY bed in my house on Porter Street, as I often did. I was stirring. I heard the phone ring and thought, *How strange, at this hour.* I made my way downstairs and into the kitchen. My mother was sitting at the table with her head on the table.

"Ma, who called? What happened? Is everything all right?" I knew everything was not all right.

She picked up her head and looked at me, her face soaked with tears.

"Daddy just called. They found Salvatore dead last night."

I turned to stone. I didn't react, I didn't scream or cry or fall on the floor and faint. I just turned to stone.

I remember that she wanted me to sit by her, but I didn't want to sit. I didn't want to do anything but withdraw. I just wanted to shrink away and disappear. I told her I was okay and then went and sat in the living room in front of the window.

There I sat for five days. I didn't move for five days. I didn't eat, I didn't drink, I didn't go to the bathroom, I didn't sleep in my bed, I didn't wash or brush my teeth—I just sat and cat-napped. Every once in a while I would awaken and they'd be there and I would ask them to just leave me alone. They were very worried but I couldn't help them.

My brother Ralph came home from New York. He asked me if I wanted to go to the funeral the next day. He said, "I will take you, I will stay with you, you won't do this alone."

I began to come out of my stupor then, but had not yet cried. "Ralph, I could never ever go to his funeral and participate as one of the crowd. I could never ever show my emotions, my feelings, my devastation, in front of so many people I might not even know. I feel like the widow. I am the widow. I only want to see him at the funeral home alone. No church. No cemetery. It's just not possible for me."

So that morning—September 20, 1984—we prepared ourselves and got to the funeral home by eight, hoping to have our own private session with him, but the funeral director told us that the room was closed until family arrived. We sat and waited. Thank God the first to arrive was Aunt Antoinette, Sal's father's sister, whom I loved and adored. We just collapsed into each other, howling. I was finally able to let it all go without any filters. She did too. We stood together, just each of us howling in a big hug. She said, "Come on, let's go see him," and we walked into the room together, holding each other.

I've ten billion words and none for that moment. Walking into that hall and seeing him dead in a coffin. I walked to the front of the room clutching Antoinette. I remember letting go of her and quickening my pace until I fell onto him. I just threw myself onto him and almost picked him up out of that box, still howling. All I did was howl uncontrollably. I remember rubbing my face on his stone-cold skin. I just kissed and kissed and kissed him, and then she was next to me. She was kissing him too and we were howling together. I couldn't turn away. I stayed right there, alone, crying and begging him over and over not to ever leave me.

After a long while I felt arms around my shoulders, gently pulling me away. It was Ralph. "Okay, enough now. Come on. It's over now. Come on. Let's go. Come on."

I remember standing up straight in front of Sal and looking at him, with Ralphie's hands on my shoulders, and thinking, *This is the last time I will see him. I will never see my Salvatore again.*

I froze on the spot, and then Ralph turned me around and led me away.

Do you understand that the hardest thing I have ever done in my whole fucking life was to turn away from that coffin? Nothing that has ever happened to me has ever been more difficult than turning away from him in that moment, and I do not believe that anything I will ever live will be as or more difficult.

When I turned and opened my eyes, the first person I saw was his sister and all I remember is falling into her and screaming. I remember holding her very tightly and I just screamed and screamed and screamed. We exchanged no words. Just held each other. While she cried, I screamed, and after a few moments we let go and I saw no one else, said nothing to anyone else. With Ralph's hands on my shoulders I let myself be led out of that room. *I will never see him again. I will never see him again. I will never see him again.*

Then we were out on Broad Street and I remember thinking, *How strange that the sun is shining. How strange that it is only nine o'clock in the morning and I feel as though I could sleep now for a hundred years.*

Ralph said, "On some level, you should be relieved. Please be at peace knowing that this is where it ends. You never have to wonder anymore where and how and when it will all end. You've arrived at the end."

And you know what? In a very strange way, those thoughts gave me great comfort. Still, I had no idea that the real winter of my life had just begun.

He drove me home and I took off my dress. It was two years before I would ever really "dress" again. Oh, yes, I went to work and went through the motions of life, day after day, but I couldn't wait to be home and in my pajamas. For two years I completely pulled back from the world and everyone in it, including my closest and dearest friends.

THIRTY-ONE

*I*T'S *1990 AND I'M living in Queen Village, in Philadelphia, in an apartment and neighborhood I love. I feel totally comfortable and at home here. I have a cheap little shit-brown Toyota Corolla that's, in those days, about ten years old, but I love it. One night it gets stolen from right in front of my door.*

I discover it gone and am bereft. I call the police and they come and they say, "Toyotas are very desirable. You'll never see this little car again." But, still, it's important for me to search and I ask them to do so. A few nights later, here's the dream:

I am sitting on the front porch of Sal's house at the shore and I'm really sad, wondering why anyone would take an old, beaten-up brown Toyota. Suddenly I hear beeping and I look up and it's Sal, driving my little Toyota. He's shouting out the window: "Stop crying! Stop worrying about the car! Look! I got the car! And I had it washed for you and even had it painted white for you! Stop crying!"

I do. Sort of.

Six weeks or so pass. I've almost forgotten the car—and then I get a phone call. "Oh, hi, this is so-and-so calling from such-and-such garage in Kensington. Seems your car has been parked out here in front of my garage for about six weeks and it really is blocking my driveway."

"Oh my God, I say, oh my God, you have my little brown Toyota!"

"Yes, I think I do, although it seems to be white because of all the snow on it."

THIRTY-TWO

I BELIEVE THAT SAL KNEW all of the "truths" in the end. I know that beyond any doubt at all because of that final time we saw each other and spent the whole night talking out on my front porch. He knew everything—I believe he had an epiphany of sorts regarding every single important aspect of his life.

I believe, too, that he knew he was going to die, even if he wasn't fully conscious of it. He had a very old-world soul. He believed in how that life should be approached and lived and he believed that you must be loyal to it and follow its rules.

The two most weighted things he said to me that August night were these: "I have nothing left. I have no one."

And: "I am so sorry I didn't listen to you. I see now that you were right—you were always right about everything and everyone. Now, don't ask me any questions." That night, he cried as much as I did.

I have forgiven him everything. He put himself down on his knees in front of me that night, and I knew that he meant with all of his heart every single word he said. On that night I got all of the real him—the Sal so very few of us knew, the Sal I had loved for sixteen years.

When we were younger, he got away with what he got away with only because I let him. I did not and do not now care what anyone thinks of him or of me or whether or not anyone else forgives him or me. I only care about my heart and his heart.

I work hard to this day on forgiving all of them—all of the people who were behind what happened to him because in truth, it was that world that killed him. This is what always happens in that world and to the people who are part of it. I look today at his best friend and my heart breaks for him. I house no rancor, no anger or rage, no vindictive feelings toward him at all. I know he suffered and I know he still suffers and I know he will suffer forever because, every night before he drifts off to sleep, I am certain he thinks, *I lost the greatest friend anyone could ever have and I am sorry for that.* I believe that it is true that a man already on the ground should never be kicked.

I dare anyone to make me feel fear. I fear *nothing* and no one in this life. A beautiful thing, that. No matter what happens to me, I know he is always right next to me. When I awaken in the next world, his is the first face I will see. So, fear—fear what?

THIRTY-THREE

*I*T IS A BRILLIANTLY *sunny day and I am walking up a hill. The grass under my feet is absolutely perfect, thick and very green. I am carrying a large white cake box and in it is a chocolate-raspberry layer cake that I bought for Salvatore. When I get to the top of the hill, in the distance I see more beautiful green hills and lots of people taking the sun or playing volleyball or soccer. A very bucolic, happy place. I look for him everywhere, among all of the people I see, but he isn't anywhere to be found. Then a man lying in the sun says, "Oh, hi. Are you looking for Sal?" I say that I am.*

"Oh, he's been waiting for you. He just went to get his bag and said for me to tell you he'll catch up with you in a few minutes. Just wait for him."

THIRTY-FOUR

September 14, 2013

Twenty-nine years since you've gone and I brought you roses.

I brought you roses today to remind you of how much I love you and always will

to honor what you have always meant to me and what you will always mean

life is long

and, if we live it right, it is rich and joyful and full of love

but

am I allowed, please, to have this moment of digression?

am I allowed to remember that morning and those days when I had to accept that you were gone you were the best friend, lover, brother, teacher, father, child, life partner, all of everything I could have ever wished for in one person... even now, after all this time, accepting you are gone is still so hard and I confront this loss every day with thoughts of you and things we lived

you are the light that never dims, the longing that doesn't cease, and the love that never diminishes

always

THIRTY-FIVE

VERY TIME ONE OF the old friends has a child who marries, a grandchild is born, or any other major milestone get marked on that road of life, my initial reaction is always overwhelming joy. But then that joy flips to its other side—the poignancy of experiencing the moment with one of Sal's friends when he's not here. I think of the magnitude of what was stolen from him and, yes, from me, and from his nieces who never got to know him. In the joy of the moment I find myself once again in mourning—mourning not really for him but on his behalf, for what he has personally lost. I just let the tears flow, for him and with him, and think that this will pass, will just get added to the life he never had the privilege to live.

I think of what we wanted, our dreams, the kids we wanted and the hopes we had, and it is so very hard to let go, let alone forget.

And so it goes and goes, and then my son Luca needs a black suit for a "formal" party and I can't tie his necktie and I wish Sal were here to help my son, because I don't know what to do with a necktie, let alone how to make him a man.

I live as best I can, feeling every inch of the way that I am flying solely by the seat of my pants and by the grace of God, wishing that I still had Sal's hand to hold onto as I go.

THIRTY-SIX

I DREAM THAT LUCA IS *a fat little tiny ball of a baby strapped to my chest in a carrier and we are walking around Rome. I walk into a big bar to have a coffee and see Sal in the back room hanging with some guys. They all look first at me and then at him and they smile. Sal and I just look at each other but don't smile or speak.*

Then I am walking across the bridge toward my old neighborhood and there, in Trastevere, it is the annual Festa di Noiantri. There are tons of people everywhere. The atmosphere is very festive and I see lots of people I know. I spot Sal's face in the crowd two more times on my way home, always smiling, always in my field of vision but always silent.

EPILOGUE

O N SEPTEMBER 20, 1984, the day Sal was buried, I began a slow, silent walk deep into myself.

I grieved and cried and cried and grieved endlessly. I smoked a lot, drank a lot, stayed home alone with my cat, and stared into space and thought. What I came to understand is that grief is sometimes far bigger and stronger than we are; try as we might to shove it off our hearts, we quickly realize that it's like an ant trying to push an elephant off its lap. I was totally incapable of fighting it. I simply allowed that grief to take root inside me and become the biggest part of me because of how utterly powerless I felt in its face. I accepted this and fully surrendered to it. Years later I would realize that there was no price for having learned this lesson: When you make an agreement of acceptance with your terrifically shattered heart, then and only then will it be permitted to receive the light—any light—and only then can it begin to heal. As Kahlil Gibran said, "The deeper that sorrow carves into your being, the more joy you can contain."

On the day that I once again heard birds sing and noticed that the sun really does shine no matter what, I also realized that I had a choice—I could indulge to stay in that place of deep mourning forever or I could choose to live and live big, as he lived and as he would wish for me to live. The magnitude of the loss I had suffered is what eventually brought me to understand that living life fully, without any fear and with a heart full of love, is the only reason we are here. I realized that there is nothing more important in life than forming and cultivating deeply loving relationships and a big happiness that is only meant to be shared. I realized that I cannot tolerate people who complain; I cannot tolerate people who are disloyal to their friends; I cannot tolerate greed, materialism, or the love of money in any form; and I cannot tolerate evil or envy in anyone, in any way, to any level, at all. I cannot see violence in films—especially if someone is shot in the head, as he was—twice. Another effect of the aftermath of my loss and my journey through it is that weddings are hard for me because each young happy couple is us; baptisms are equally as hard for me because the child being presented to God is ours; funerals are nearly impossible for me because that closed casket always contains his remains. Thirty years later, after I was finally able to look back and excavate the deepest inner reaches of my heart, I realized that I had a story to tell and that it would be my life's deepest and most important exhale.

There's a poem by Veronica A. Shoffstall that reads:

After a while you learn the subtle difference
Between holding a hand and chaining a soul,
And you learn that love doesn't mean possession
And company doesn't mean security.
And you begin to learn that kisses aren't contracts
And presents aren't promises
And you begin to accept your defeats
With your head up and your eyes ahead
With the grace of a woman, not the grief of a child.
And you learn to build all your roads on today,
Because tomorrow's ground is too uncertain for plans
And futures have a way of falling down in midflight.
After a while you learn
That even sunshine burns if you get too much.
So you plant your own garden and decorate your own soul,
Instead of waiting for someone to bring you flowers.
And you learn that you really can endure. . .
That you really are strong.
And you really do have worth. And you learn and learn. . .
With every goodbye, you learn.

This is what it was and still is for me.

Since the time of Sal's death, I have had three very significant relationships, I moved to Italy where I lived for almost a dozen years, had a child at forty-one years of age on my own in Rome, moved to

New York when my child was almost seven to work as a public-relations representative for my supremely brilliant brother, Ralph, and, after eight years there, moved back to Philadelphia to my family home, only several feet away from Sal's front door, where our story bloomed and where everything had all played out. Was it a coincidence that I felt compelled to finally put pen to paper at that point? I think not. The truth is that he walked right in behind me, sat down in my living room, and said, "Okay, are you now ready to assess all of this?" I was. And I did.

Where I am today is here: No matter where my life goes from here, I know and understand and accept that, for me, there will never be another Salvatore. It simply wouldn't be possible for me to have another story with someone that is as wide and as deep and as full of extraordinary life experiences as our story was and still is. Also, being that I'm looking at turning sixty in a few years, I couldn't help but have an epiphany of sorts about his importance in my life. You see, I never intended for him to become the centerpiece of my life—but circumstances and events and my heart brought me to the understanding that he is and has always been just that. For me there is only him, and I know with all my heart that where he is, he waits for me and looks forward to the day when I can join him. I know and am solidly aware that, for him, now, our story and all of its dramas and passions, horrors and comedies, treacheries and emotions are but a mere blink of his eye. That's fine, because I am still, to quote Ram Dass, "a spiritual being having a human experience," whereas Sal now exists on a far higher plane. Where he is there is only eternity, and it is eternity that we shall have—but only after I am finished here. For now, I take enormous comfort in knowing that we never left each other. There was nothing ever left unsaid between us, we never said, "Goodbye, I don't love you anymore, this is over" to each other, we never ended our relationship in any way. He died knowing that despite all that had happened between us and to us, my heart still belonged to him, as his still belonged to me. I know that he is with me every single step of the way and my life is, in any case, rich and full and beautiful and overflowing with extraordinary love.

Rosina
September 2014

THANK YOU. . .

To Lisa Radano, great friend, brilliant writer, and creative thinker, who said, "Just hold my hand, I will guide you"

To Sara Canuso, a powerhouse of an entrepreneur and professional, who said, "Walk down this road and you'll find what you need"—and I did

To Judy Weintraub, sent to me by Sara, who made it real

To Sarah Grey, who fell in love with our story and treated it with reverence and respect

and

To all of those who spoke with me, opening up their hearts, sharing our memories and our enormous love for him.

Thank you all, with much love from the bottom of my heart.

ABOUT THE AUTHOR

Rosina Rucci was born and raised in South Philadelphia. A graduate degree in Journalism from that city's Temple University lead to work in Rome, Italy where she served as Promotions Manager for the children's channel of the ORBIT Satellite Television and Radio Network. An extraordinary twelve years of life in Rome gave her knowledge of the city, fluency in the Italian language, and her adored son Luca who was born there in 1997. Though South Philadelphia is her beloved birthplace, Italy is her true home and though leaving it in 2003 was difficult, she was thrilled at the chance to work alongside her brother, renowned fashion designer, Ralph Rucci of New York City, as Director of Communications. She has since returned to South Philadelphia, where she currently resides, where her son attends school and where this deeply personal story was born.

Made in the USA
Middletown, DE
29 September 2023

39769039R00076